The Rockabilly Legends

They Called It Rockabilly Long Before They Called It Rock and Roll

HAL•LEONARD

WHY DO I LIKE THIS KIND OF MUSIC? FIRST OF ALL, IT HAS A GOOD BEAT; IT'S NOT COMPLICATED; IT'S NOT TRYING TO SELL ME SOMETHING; IT'S NOT TRYING TO STRAIGHTEN MY MORALS OUT OR SCREW MY MORALS UP.

— BUDDY KNOX, WEST TEXAS FIFTIES ROCK AND ROLL-ROCKABILLY LEGEND

ROCKABILLY IS TAKEN FROM SOME OF THOSE OLD GOSPEL SONGS, BLACK SPIRITUALS, THE DELTA BLUES, BLUE GRASS, COUNTRY AND HILLBILLY. YOU KNOW, IT'S THE WHOLE THING. ROCKABILLY COVERS IT ALL.

—TILLMAN FRANKS, SONGWRITER, MUSICIAN, PERSONAL MANAGER, PROMOTER

Published by Hal Leonard Corporation
7777 Bluemound Road
P.O. Box 13819
Milwaukee, WI 53213

Trade Book Division Editorial Offices
19 West 21st Street Suite 201
New York, New York 10010

Library of Congress Cataloging-in-Publication Data
Naylor, Jerry, 1939-
   The Rockabilly Legends : They Called It Rockabilly Long Before It Was Called Rock and Roll/
   Jerry Naylor and Steve Halliday. -- 1st ed.
      p. cm.
   ISBN-13: 978-1-4234-2042-2   ISBN-10: 1-4234-2042-x
   1. Rockabilly music--History and criticism. I. Halliday, Steve, 1957- II. Title.

ML3535.N39 2007
781.66--dc22

                                              2006032236

Printed in China through Colorcraft Ltd., Hong Kong
First Edition

Hal Leonard books are available at your local bookstore, or you may order through Music Dispatch at
1-800-637-2852 or www.musicdispatch.com

CONTENTS

Introduction   10

Chapter 1   The Accidental Big Bang   26

Chapter 2   Three Days That Changed the World   56

Chapter 3   It's In the Soul   116

Chapter 4   The Only Music We Wanted to Make   148

Chapter 5   Fellas, We Hardly Knew Ye   202

Epilogue   276

Design by Scott Petersen and Jonah Nolde

To Pamela:
Your forty-one years of faithful love made this writing possible.

ROCK★

INTRODUCTION: THEY CALLED IT ROCKABILLY LONG BEFORE THEY CALLED IT ROCK AND ROLL

You may call it "the birth of rock and roll," "early rock," "foundational rock and roll," "the beginning of rock," or perhaps even "fifties rock and roll." But whatever name you put to this 1950s infectious, raw musical genre—a phenomenon that changed world culture and influenced all music that followed—you simply must know that Carl Perkins, Mr. "Blue Suede Shoes" himself, described it best.

When asked to explain his musical creations, Carl took a deep breath and with his distinctive Southern drawl definitively exclaimed, "Well, they called it *Rockabilly* long before they called it *rock and roll!*" And friends, if Carl Perkins calls it Rockabilly, then it was and still is ROCKABILLY!

With his 1956 classic recording, Carl Perkins defined and established Rockabilly music as the necessary precursor to rock and roll. "Blue Suede Shoes" holds the distinction of being the first million-selling Rockabilly record in history. Carl's original recording of the song was also the first in history to top the country, rhythm & blues, and pop charts and remained on the national charts for twenty-one weeks. The success of "Blue Suede Shoes" propelled Perkins into rock and roll royalty; in 1987 he was inducted into the Rock and Roll Hall of Fame and Museum. (You'll read more about his legendary exploits a little later.)

The fact is, seven of the Rockabilly Legends celebrated in this book are inductees into the Rock and Roll Hall of Fame and Museum. Elvis Presley, Buddy Holly, and Jerry Lee Lewis got things moving when they became members of the first class, in 1986. Carl Perkins and Roy Orbison joined them the next year, while Johnny Cash followed them in 1992; Gene Vincent took his well-deserved place in 1998. The Johnny Burnette Trio, Buddy Knox, and The Crickets are all on a short list of Rockabilly Legends destined for future induction into the Rock and Roll Hall of Fame and Museum.

AND YES, CARL, IT'S IMPORTANT TO SAY IT ONE MORE TIME:
"THEY CALLED IT ROCKABILLY LONG BEFORE THEY CALLED IT ROCK AND ROLL!"

ROCKABILLY CHANGED MY LIFE

I was only fifteen years old when an untamed force unlike anything I had ever experienced permanently altered the direction of my professional career. It was 1954, a year destined to go down in music history as pure magic.

When I wasn't attending classes at Lake View High School in San Angelo, Texas, I performed as a singer wherever someone would have me. Most Friday and Saturday nights, my band and I performed the best tunes of Hank Williams, Ernest Tubb, Lefty Frizzell, T. Texas Tyler, Bill Monroe, and Bob Wills in the local beer joints. I considered it creative nourishment: poignant hillbilly country music, sung live and with passion in the dank, smoky honky-tonks where we played—often while dodging flying beer bottles! Although I was not legally old enough even to enter these joints, the life experiences I had there fundamentally ripened me. They also filled a deep hunger raging within my soul.

I was born to sing, and shortly after I entered this world, my dear, sweet mother (who played piano in our small country church) placed me at her feet, just under the edge of the old upright piano, while she pounded out those great gospel "shape-notes" into a passionate pattern of spiritual excellence. So it should surprise no one that, during my teen years, my Saturday night-honkytonk singing quickly evolved into Sunday morning and Sunday night church singing. Instinctively and with equal passion, I belted out "I'll Fly Away" and other grand old Southern gospel testimonials from the hymnal of the Carlsbad, Texas, Southern Baptist Church.

I first heard African-American spirituals and delta blues at age thirteen, and by 1954, I was singing with an all-black trio—Robert T. Smith and His Men of Blues—in Negro clubs around San Angelo. Those places knew no racial divide, no hint of segregation. This was the Mississippi delta blues, meant for all people—even us young white boys from West Texas.

I still feel riveted by Jerry Lee Lewis's stories of how he and his cousins, Jimmy Swaggart and Mickey Gilley, fed their piano-playing passion at the expense of defying copperhead snakes. At a very early age they crawled far up under the old wooden floor boards of black Pentecostal churches around Ferriday, Louisiana, settling directly under the pounding rhythm of the piano player's feet. Each of them shadow-played along on their make-believe pianos in the moist dirt, carefully following the pounding spirituals on the keyboard above. While lying on their bellies in the Louisiana dirt, they all got literally baptized with a flood of sounds and rhythms of black Southern gospel music at its very richest.

It was this foundation that bequeathed to each of us the vibrant musical patterns to come. In fact, Rockabilly music never would have developed at all without Southern gospel. *All* of us started in church. We may have drifted pretty far away for a time, but eventually nearly all of us came back. Church is where we experienced the real meaning of singing and praising, and from church we incorporated gospel influences into our routine performances and creative writing. So whether it's in church or on the concert stage, when the music gets to rocking, the hands get to clapping, and the crowd gets to praising, that's pure heaven on earth.

I KNEW FOR A FACT THAT MY LIFE WOULD NEVER BE THE SAME

RADIO LENDS A HAND

Radio also played a critical role in my career, as it did for each of the Rockabilly Legends. From age fourteen, I worked as a disc jockey on KPEP radio in San Angelo, one of the first stations in America to program country music as a full-time format. Until then, just about every radio station featured "block" formats: diverse national and local daily programming that included drama, news, and various genres of music ranging from big band to classical and hillbilly. And on one blistering hot West Texas July afternoon, my world changed forever.

The very moment I picked up the newly arrived 45 RPM vinyl record—the one with a bright yellow label, a large black rooster, and the bold letters S-U-N on it—the "Rockabilly virus" seized my soul. I literally shook as I gently placed the record onto the control room turntable, carefully eased the stylus down, and opened my microphone. As the booming Martin guitar churned out a new and magical kind of pushy rhythm, I announced, "This is the first record release from a brand-new singer down in Memphis, Tennessee. His name is Elvis Presley. AHHH, *That's All Right (Mama)!*" At that moment Elvis took over the airwaves, singing, *"Wellll, that's all right now, Mama, that's all right for you, that's all right now, Mama, any way you doooo, well that's all right!"*

I HAD NEVER HEARD ANYTHING LIKE IT. I CLICKED OFF THE ANNOUNCER'S MIC, AND THIS UNIQUE, RAW, ORIGINAL MUSIC REVERBERATED OFF THE WALLS OF KPEP'S CONTROL ROOM. I STOOD UP AND BEGAN TO SHOUT AND DANCE AROUND. I TURNED UP THE MONITORS EVEN LOUDER AND YELLED WITH UNCONTROLLABLE EXCITEMENT,

"THIS IS IT! THIS IS WHAT I'VE BEEN WAITING FOR! THIS IS GREAT!!"

AT THAT VERY MOMENT, I KNEW FOR A FACT THAT MY LIFE WOULD NEVER BE THE SAME. I WANTED TO RUN DOWN THE ROAD, SHOUTING TO EVERYBODY, "THE WORLD OF MUSIC HAS CHANGED FOREVER!"

WHAT MADE ROCKABILLY SO UNIQUE?

I THINK IT COMES DOWN TO SEVERAL UNIQUE CHARACTERISTICS: A "PUSHY," FAT RHYTHM GUITAR;
THE ELECTRIFYING MAGNETISM OF A GUTSY, RHYTHMIC LEAD GUITAR; THE BLISTERING SLAP OF AN
UPRIGHT BASS FIDDLE; PLUS ALL OF THESE ELEMENTS SWIMMING IN A MAN-MADE LAKE
OF "TAPE-DELAY ECHO."

IN OTHER WORDS, THE MAGIC OF ROCKABILLY ERUPTS AS MUCH IN THE DETAIL OF THE MUSIC AS
IN THE LYRICS OF THE SONG AND THE SINGER'S PERFORMANCE.

ROCKABILLY EVOLVED INTO A DISTINCT FORM IN A VERY SMALL WINDOW OF TIME. IT BEGAN IN 1953,
AND BY 1959 IT HAD CLEAR DEFINITION—JUST SIX SHORT YEARS! STILL, THE EXPLOSIVE MUSICAL
ORIGINALITY THAT ROCKED THOSE YEARS CONTINUES TO EXERT A TREMENDOUS INFLUENCE TODAY;
JUST LISTEN TO ALMOST EVERY CONTEMPORARY ROCK AND ROLL, POP, OR COUNTRY MUSIC ARTIST.
WITHIN THEIR MUSIC, FIFTIES ROCKABILLY STILL LIVES!

A "PUSI

THE ELECTRIFYING MAGNETISM OF A GUTSY RHYTHMIC LEAD GUITAR

BLISTERING SLAP
UPRIGHT BASS FIDDLE

ALL OF THESE ELEMENTS
MING
IN A MAN-MADE LAKE OF
TAPE-DELAY
ECHO

The fifties were a decade of change. Young people around the world who know about this period of history only vicariously can still relate to it as an exciting time of wild and reckless abandon. Everywhere, it seemed, people were shedding everything old for new experiments and fresh experiences.

A DECADE

But beneath the frivolity and tinsel of a decade that saw millions gyrating with hula hoops and wearing funny glasses at the movies, "The Fabulous Fifties" made possible a growing awareness of change that ignited the Civil Rights Movement, created a space program, and nurtured a "King." The babies born during the Great Depression and World War II came of age in the fifties. This groundbreaking decade gave us the interstate highway system, network television, new developments in entertainment, music, art and literature . . . and even the distinctly American experiment of junk food.

OF CHANGE

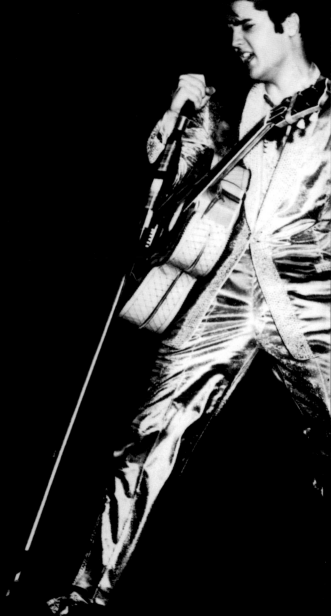

The fifties were an era charged with vitality and complexity, an often turbulent time set against the backdrop of an energetic economic boom laden with fads, stars, and tragedies. History-making moments and trends all got exaggerated within themselves. The Korean War erupted as the first major East-West conflict; Senator Joseph Mc-Carthy waged war on Communists (and on some of America's most creative icons); Dwight Eisenhower became president, presiding over an eerie national calm from his office on the Potomac; the Supreme Court declared segregation in the schools unconstitutional; the Civil Rights Movement began its long march under the courageous leadership of Martin Luther King, Jr.;

the Soviet Union's *Sputnik* satellite scared the United States into launching its own aggressive space program; television became an American way of life, threatening the motion picture industry and changing family lifestyles; drive-in movies, 3-D and giant-screen Cinerama films became a national sensation; James Dean, Marlon Brando, Marilyn Monroe, and other media darlings entertained the country; and a powerful new movement in music began to change the world, led by a young truck driver from Tupelo, Mississippi, who became the "King of Rockabilly"!

HALF A CENTURY LATER, ROCKABILLY MUSIC IS VERY MUCH ALIVE AND WELL, AS EVIDENCED IN OUR ANTHOLOGY, THE ROCKABILLY LEGENDS: THEY CALLED IT ROCKABILLY LONG BEFORE THEY CALLED IT ROCK AND ROLL.

THIS LONG OVERDUE TRIBUTE REVEALS THE DEEP RESPECT I HAVE FOR THE PIONEERS OF THIS POWERFUL GENRE OF MUSIC. I FEEL VERY BLESSED TO HAVE KNOWN, WORKED WITH, AND BECOME FRIENDS WITH MOST OF THESE GREAT LEGENDS—AND I'M VERY PROUD TO HAVE THIS OPPORTUNITY TO SHARE THESE PERSONAL MEMORIES WITH YOU.

THIS IS OUR STORY.

THE ACCIDENTAL BIG BANG

ROCK-A-BILLY: (N.) AN EMOTIONALLY INTENSE AND RHYTHMIC BLEND OF [HILLBILLY] COUNTRY MUSIC, BLUEGRASS, RHYTHM AND BLUES, SOUTHERN GOSPEL, AND AFRICAN-AMERICAN SPIRITUALS. ORIGINALLY PERFORMED BY WHITE MUSICIANS FROM THE MID-SOUTHERN REGION OF THE UNITED STATES. CHARACTERIZED BY ASSERTIVE, CONFIDENT SINGLE VOCAL PERFORMANCE, MODERATELY FAST TEMPOS, AND THREE TO FOUR MUSICIANS USING ACOUSTIC RHYTHM GUITAR, UPRIGHT "SLAP" BASS, ELECTRIC LEAD GUITAR, AND SOMETIMES DRUMS. DISCERNIBLE STUDIO ECHO-EFFECTS ENHANCE THE RECORDINGS.

CRAIG MORRISON IN *GO CAT GO! ROCKABILLY MUSIC AND ITS MAKERS*

Like many slang definitions of various types of music—think of boogie-woogie, Dixieland, and swing—no one seems to know who actually coined the word *Rockabilly.*

The only fact on which most everyone agrees is that Rockabilly music was born on the sweltering night of July 5, 1954, when a young truck driver turned struggling singer was nervously horsing around during a coffee break of a demo session at a tiny Memphis recording studio.

THAT YOUNG MISSISSIPPIAN LED THE ROCKABILLY EXPLOSION—A POWERFUL NEW TYPE OF MUSIC THAT IGNITED YOUNG PEOPLE ALL ACROSS THE NATION WHILE AT THE SAME TIME CAUSING PANIC AMONG PARENTS AND PREACHERS. BUT HE NEVER WOULD HAVE CAUGHT ANYONE'S ATTENTION AT ALL WITHOUT THE HELP OF A CREATIVE, ECCENTRIC BUSINESSMAN NAMED SAM PHILLIPS.

THE ROLE OF SAM PHILLIPS

Sam Phillips, a former radio announcer from Memphis, Tennessee, saw the future through the mighty changes of the fifties and acted on his vision. With an uncontrollable passion for black boogie and blues music, Sam felt driven to spend every night soaking up round-the-clock entertainment at the nightspots and from the street musicians of Memphis's Beale Street. With limited finances, he began recording many of these black singers at his small Memphis Recording Services Studio.

From 1951 to 1953, Phillips achieved limited success selling these works to record companies in Memphis, Chicago, and Los Angeles, but he gained little financial return for his efforts.

Still, Phillips remained focused on his vision. While most black record companies of the day wanted to groom an artist to break through the segregated barriers of white radio in order to reach a larger audience, Sam longed to find a white singer-performer who could do his act with the same soulful sound and moves of the black entertainers he loved so much.

"Everyone knew that I was just a little struggling cat down here trying to develop new and hopefully different artists," Sam once said, "and get some freedom in music and tap some resources and people that weren't being tapped."

To shore up his financial bottom line, Sam began recording anything, anywhere, anytime—weddings, funerals, country music artists. Scotty Moore, a newcomer to Memphis and lead guitar player for a country music group called the Starlight Wranglers, found out that Sam had a recording service. So he went to see Sam.

Scotty probed Phillips about where his fledgling recording studio was going. Sam finally admitted that he wasn't sure, but he had a vision for something new, a fresh kind of music. "I will know it when I hear it," Phillips declared emphatically.

The pair became close friends through making a record together. Practically every day, Scotty went by the studio, and if Sam wasn't busy recording someone for pay or audition, the two of them would go next door to Mrs. Taylor's restaurant and have coffee, just to chitchat and talk about the business.

Meanwhile, nineteen-year-old Elvis Presley lived with his parents in a federal housing district near Phillips's small studio. The young Elvis, desperate to become a professional singer, spent much of his spare time at local black churches, listening to and observing their powerful performers. He also befriended the popular white Southern gospel Blackwood Brothers quartet. When Presley visited Sam's studio and paid $3.98 (plus tax) to record "My Happiness" and "That's When the Heartaches Begin" for his mother's birthday, Sam's secretary, Marion Keisker, made a note of his address and telephone number. She sensed "something" in the boy's style of singing and wanted to make her boss aware of him.

Over the next ten months, Elvis suffered disappointment after disappointment as he sang in (and always lost) many Memphis-area amateur contests. At the same time, Scotty Moore became displeased with his country swing band's lack of success. He constantly reminded Sam that he liked to play blues and jazz and was open to playing new music styles. Sam liked Scotty because, unlike most musicians, Scotty paid attention to details, as Sam himself did.

In the meantime, Marion continued to remind her boss about the young dark-haired boy who had come in months before to record birthday ballads for his mother. Sam usually grunted back that he would think about it—but the subject never came up unless Marion mentioned it.

On one hot Saturday morning, however—July 3, 1954—Scotty Moore, eager to improve his business relationship with Sam, showed up at the studio and nagged Sam about calling "that Presley boy" for an audition. Phillips, frustrated that he had no patrons wanting to record even a wedding or funeral, finally broke down and told Marion to dig out Presley's number and give it to Scotty.

That afternoon Scotty called the Presley home, only to find that Elvis had left for the movies. A few hours later, Presley returned Scotty's call and the two set a time to meet the next day.

The following afternoon, the thermometer registered a sizzling one hundred degrees when Elvis showed up at Scotty's small house; but disappointingly, he gave a less than sizzling audition. Scotty didn't care much for Elvis's renditions of the crooner ballads the young man loved so much. Bill Black, Scotty's bass player from the country band, dropped by while Elvis sang "Because of You," "I Love You Because," and "Just Because You Think You're So Pretty." As soon as Elvis left for home, Bill blasted the young singer's efforts and summed up his feelings with a dour, "He sure didn't impress me very much!"

Scotty, itching for a steady job at the recording studio, desperately wanted to please Sam and so phoned in an exaggerated report that Elvis had talent, knew a bunch of rhythm and blues songs, and that Sam absolutely should offer him an audition. Based on that glowing recommendation, Phillips told Scotty to call Elvis and he'd set up a recording audition for Monday night.

MODERN STUDIOS

MEMPHIS *Recording* SERVICE

TELEPHONE 37-7197

706 UNION AT MARSHALL

DISC   "WE RECORD ANYTHING—ANYWHERE—ANYTIME"   TAPE

"WHAT THE HELL ARE YOU GUYS DOING OUT THERE?"

THE ACCIDENT

Around the world, it's known as The Big Bang or The Accident. On July 5, 1954, music history changed forever. And a lesser-known 1940's R & B song by Arthur "Big Boy" Crudup played a major role in it.

Elvis Presley's first recording session began with a nervous trio: Scotty Moore on lead guitar, Bill Black on upright slap bass, and Elvis singing and playing rhythm guitar. They all sat around the studio trying to figure out what songs they mutually knew well enough to perform. Scotty was acutely aware that Sam could become very caustic if he felt someone was wasting his time. Unfortunately, the trio started off unimpressively with Bing Crosby's "Harbor Lights" and Ernest Tubb's "I Love You Because." When it became painfully clear that they had not improved on the Crosby or Tubb performances, they frantically searched for something else.

After some discussion they tried one more ballad, but their heart just wasn't in it. Sam, less than impressed, started rapidly pacing in the control room, revealing a growing restlessness and nearing his boiling point. The three had gone nowhere fast, and the tension level in the room had risen very high.

Around midnight, an irritated Sam was about to pull the plug and call off the whole audition. To make matters worse, Scotty and Bill had taken refuge from Sam's verbal attacks by retreating to the studio toilet. Elvis felt the horror of total abandonment.

Desperate and full of nervous energy, the young performer suddenly grabbed his guitar, locked his fingers firmly in the only chord position he knew well, and started beating the fire out of the strings while singing what little he knew of Arthur Crudup's "That's All Right (Mama)"—a *race* song he had heard on a local black rhythm and blues radio station. Ironically, some years earlier Phillips had recorded the same song.

Bill Black heard the new attempt, started laughing, joined Elvis in the studio, and began wiggling his bass fiddle around, mimicking the accelerated tempo Elvis had set. Then Scotty, who did not know the song, added his lead guitar and punched along the performance with pushy ad-lib chord fills. Bill commented, "Get that on the radio, they'll run us out of town."

But Sam yelled out, "What the hell are you guys doing out there?"

The music abruptly stopped. Worried they had landed themselves in trouble, Elvis nervously answered, "Just fooling around, Mr. Phillips."

Sam yelled back from the control room, "Well, do THAT again, but let me get this tape machine running first!"

It was a complete accident. No one planned it or expected it to happen. Out of the dark, muggy frustration of disappointment, it came. Elvis, Scotty, and Bill had created a new sound that would change all pop music to follow. Sam captured this magic on tape, added his own brand of tape delay echo, and finally realized his long-awaited vision. They had indeed coupled the excitement, soul, and performance of the black man's music and performed it in a brand-new genre that people of all races around the world would accept.

Phillips knew he had captured greatness that night on his half-inch recording tape. The "Rockabilly virus" had exploded into existence! Historians would write about the impact of this contagious, revolutionary music for decades to come, and millions would feel the impact of its infectious power.

ROCKING BLUE MOON BLUES

THE NEXT DAY, WHEN THE TRIO RETURNED TO THE STUDIO, SAM TOLD THE PUMPED UP MUSICIANS THAT THEY HAD A RECORD—WELL, HALF A RECORD, ANYWAY. THEY NOW NEEDED A B-SIDE.

Carried along by the excitement of their accidental take on "That's All Right (Mama)," they ran through several songs, awaiting the magic's return. But nothing clicked. After a long series of duds, Sam told them to take a few days to come up with something. Elvis, Scotty, and Bill remained upbeat and did a lot of clowning around. They felt sure it would happen again, that suddenly it would just click and they would have another wonderful accident. Sam didn't feel quite so sure.

Later that night, Sam called his disc jockey friend Dewey Phillips (no relation), the "Wolfman Jack" of that era in Memphis. Dewey was an unorthodox radio personality with little professional training but a big voice, wild imagination, and a huge following among both black and white listeners. Dewey listened as Sam told him he had something very unusual that he just had to hear.

Dewey, known for his "shock jock" sensationalism, always felt excited to hear anything truly different.

Sam played "That's All Right (Mama)" over and over for Dewey for more than two hours as the two men drank cheap southern whiskey and listened raptly. Dewey absolutely flipped over the new sound. Sam ran off an acetate for him and the next night the DJ played "That's All Right (Mama)" on his wildly popular *Red, Hot and Blue* radio show on WHBQ. Sam telephoned Elvis to listen, but the future legend had gone out once more to the movies. Dewey played the recording—and played it and played it. Over and over he played "That's All Right (Mama)," shouting and yelling "hoodoo jive" he made up and screaming to listeners to get on top of this wild new sound.

The telephones began ringing off the wall. Listeners drove to the studio to find out where this new sound had come from and where they could get it. "That's All Right (Mama)" became an instant hit. A feeling of ecstasy filled the air as people of all colors started dancing in the streets and on the sidewalks, listening to the song on their car radios.

Dewey soon telephoned Elvis to come down to the studio for an interview. Within minutes of the call, Elvis's parents, Gladys and Vernon, rounded up their son and drove him to the station. Elvis felt very nervous and told Dewey, "Mr. Phillips, I don't know anything about being interviewed on the radio."

"Just don't say anything dirty," Dewey sagely advised the young man.

With such unprecedented reaction from listeners, Sam knew he had to get that B-side for the record—and soon. A stampede of prospective record buyers flooded the local stores, creating initial orders for five thousand copies of the new record. Sam slapped a recording contract down in front of Elvis for his signature, and Scotty Moore executed a personal management contract with Presley.

Yet now a big problem stared the trio in the face: None of them wrote songs. So they had no choice but to find something from someone else. For two days, Elvis, Scotty, and Bill went through song after song, trying to find the elusive magic again. Nothing worked. And then, when all seemed darkest and Sam was preparing to release "That's All Right (Mama)" on both sides of the record, the trio got lucky once again.

"Blue Moon of Kentucky," a bluegrass waltz, had by 1946 become a nationwide hit for its writer and singer, Bill Monroe. It quickly became a classic country bluegrass tune, revered by the Grand Ole' Opry and handled with kid gloves. No one dared to abuse its purity of origin.

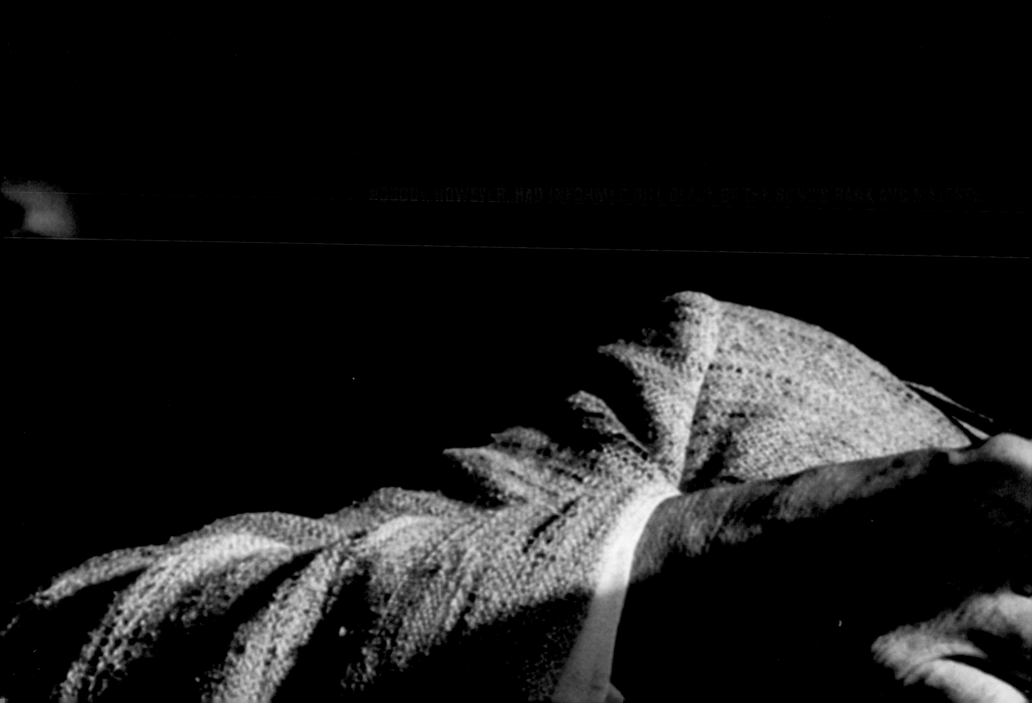

NOBODY, HOWEVER, HAD INFORMED BILL BLACK OF THE SUN'S RANK AND MAJESTY

Ten days after the "accidental" recording of "That's All Right (Mama)," the trio was back in the recording studio. In a dry moment, Bill Black jumped up, grabbed his big bass fiddle, and began viciously slapping the dog out of it and singing in a very high, almost mocking falsetto voice, *"Blue Moon of Kentucky, Justa' Keep on A Shining...."*

Elvis's eyes widened, and he quickly joined in, playfully singing with Bill and pounding on the rhythm guitar, much as he had done on "That's All Right (Mama)." Again, Scotty added his black-flavored, silky lead guitar chords—and once more the genie flew out of the bottle.

They had captured the "magic" again.

Sam Phillips, as before, stuck his head out of the door of his closetlike control room and shouted, "That's the one! That's the one! Don't lose it while I get the tape rolling!"

By the final take, a jubilant Sam shouted over and over, "BOY, that's fine, that's fine. That's a POP song now!"

With "That's All Right (Mama)," Elvis took a black blues song and sang it white. On "Blue Moon of Kentucky," he took a white bluegrass song and turned it bluesy. The trio's innovative sound then got gift-wrapped in the ocean of Sam Phillips's unique, man-made tape delay echo—and the revolution had truly begun. Rockabilly had arrived on the scene.

After one disappointing appearance at the Bon Air Club, Elvis, Scotty, and Bill got booked by Bob Neal, a local Memphis country music disc jockey, to appear with Slim Whitman at the Overton Park Shell, an outdoor amphitheater located adjacent to the Memphis zoo.

The night of the show, Elvis felt so nervous that his legs wobbled and shook uncontrollably. He wore wide-legged dress pants, and when he began to sing, his leg gyrations and nervous movements caused the young ladies in the family-oriented audience to go crazy and start screaming. Sam could hardly believe what he was seeing—and hearing.

That August, Sam packed his car full with box after box of the new records and hit the road to preach the gospel of Elvis to every promoter, disc jockey, local record distributor, and radio station in the South. Sam slept in his car most nights—partially because he was short of money and mainly because he didn't want anyone to steal those precious recordings.

When Sam returned from his promotion trip, he telephoned Jim Denny, manager of the Grand Ole' Opry in Nashville, to book Elvis on the show. Denny felt less than lukewarm about the idea and told Sam he had heard Elvis's recordings—and they just weren't fit for the Grand Ole' Opry. But Sam pressured Denny so hard that he finally agreed to book the new act on one condition: They perform only one song, "Blue Moon of Kentucky."

THE FIRST ROCKABILLY RELEASE SCREAMS

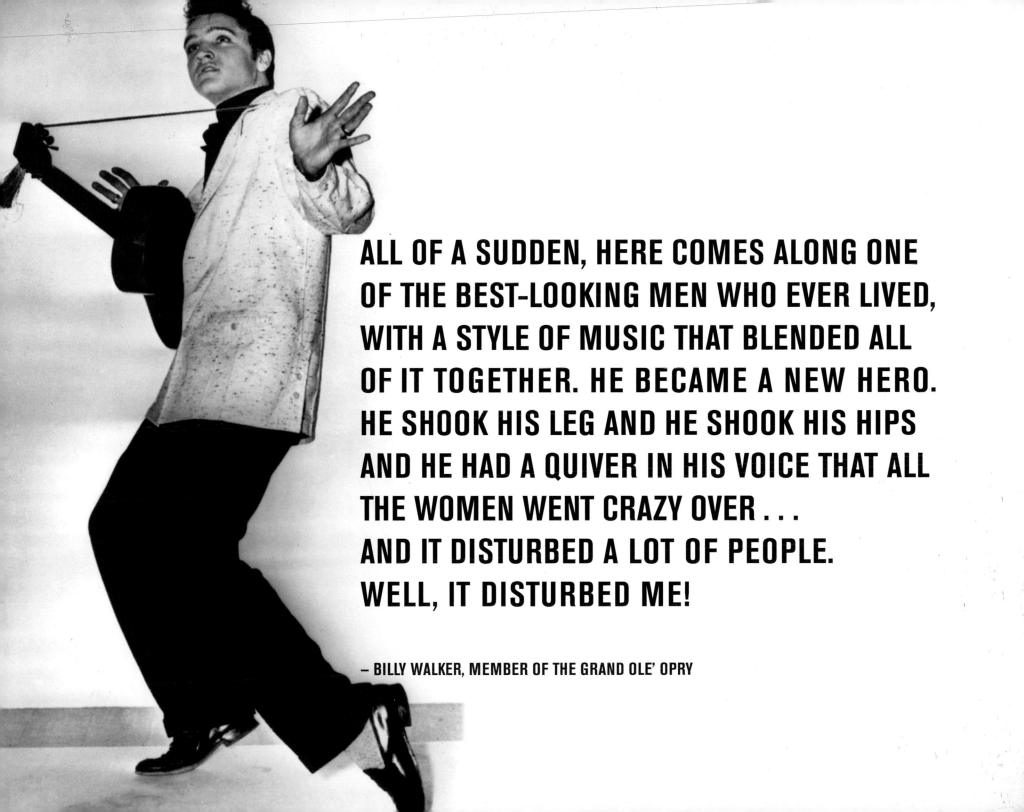

ALL OF A SUDDEN, HERE COMES ALONG ONE
OF THE BEST-LOOKING MEN WHO EVER LIVED,
WITH A STYLE OF MUSIC THAT BLENDED ALL
OF IT TOGETHER. HE BECAME A NEW HERO.
HE SHOOK HIS LEG AND HE SHOOK HIS HIPS
AND HE HAD A QUIVER IN HIS VOICE THAT ALL
THE WOMEN WENT CRAZY OVER . . .
AND IT DISTURBED A LOT OF PEOPLE.
WELL, IT DISTURBED ME!

– BILLY WALKER, MEMBER OF THE GRAND OLE' OPRY

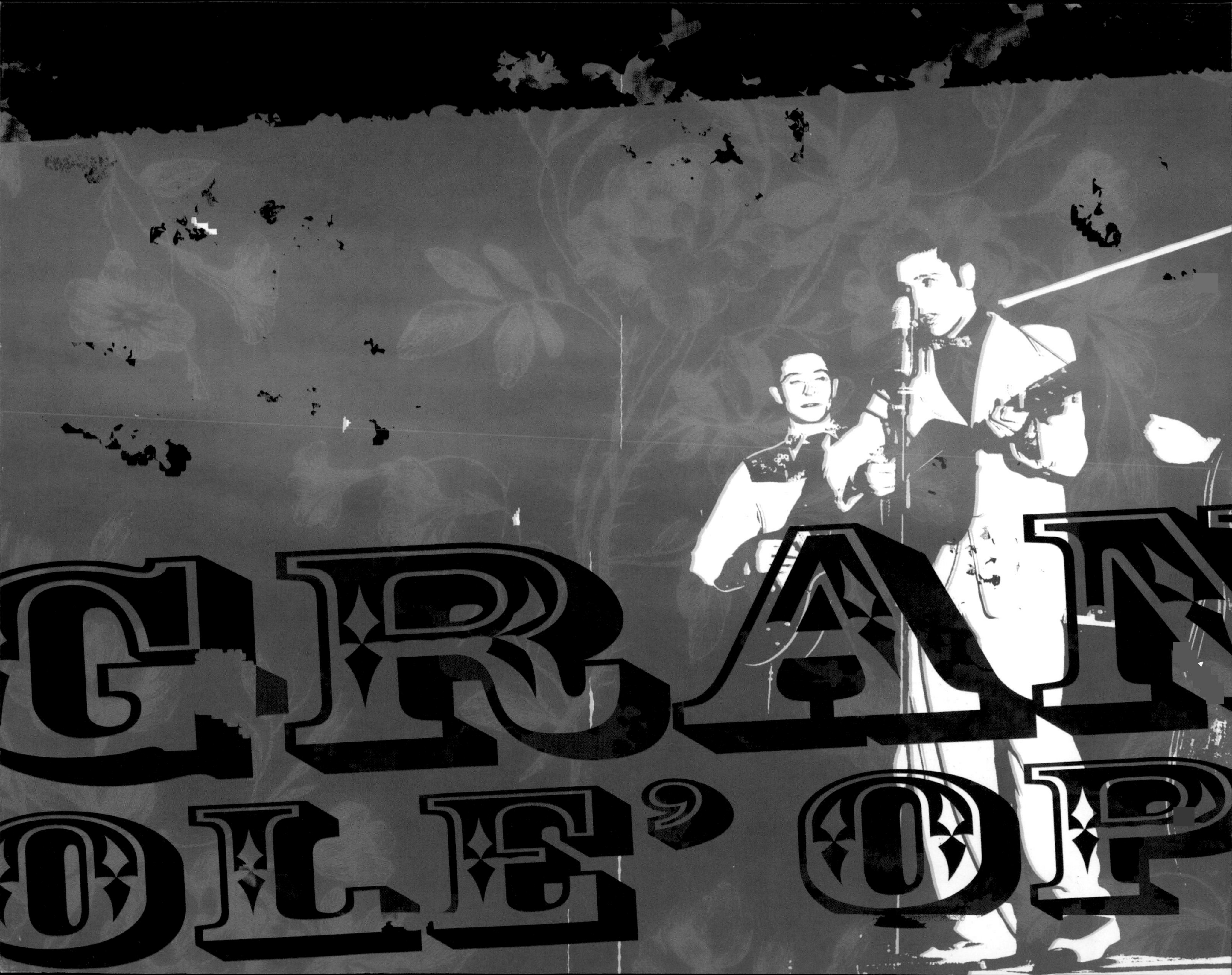
GRAN
OLE' OP

THE CONFUSED GRAND OLE' STODGY

On Saturday night, October 2, 1954—less than three months after the "That's All Right (Mama)" recording accident—Elvis Presley, Scotty Moore, and Bill Black appeared on the hallowed Ryman Auditorium stage of the Grand Ole' Opry. The place didn't exactly impress Elvis. He thought the auditorium would look a little fancier, with less of the homey gospel hall feeling that had made it so legendary.

When only three musicians arrived at the stage door, Jim Denny felt even more concerned about his decision to allow Elvis to perform. He thought from the big sound of the recording that more performers had played on the session—yet another listener snookered by Sam's slap-back echo sound. Reluctantly, he allowed the trio to go on.

Hank Snow introduced the nervous group, and the trio took the stage to little fanfare. The deathly quiet of the packed auditorium only filled the trio with more fear. When you have just one song to perform, it's do-or-die. You have little room for recovery if things don't go well—and they knew this was a very tough audience.

Elvis and the boys performed "Blue Moon of Kentucky" just as they had in the studio. The new arrangement and strange sound appeared to stun the capacity audience, but they remained cautiously polite and applauded hesitantly. Fortunately, no one started booing or hissing. On the other hand, no one screamed or went crazy as they had at the Overton Park Shell. Elvis managed to contain his shaking legs, and his stifled performance left the audience in doubt about his professional music future.

Sam's head sank as they left the alley stage door across from Tootsies Orchid Lounge. There would be no celebration for them that night; as a matter of fact, some hillbilly loyalists were ready to take the young Crown Electric truck driver to task for abusing the sacred Bill Monroe classic.

AND WHO COULD FORGET THE FINAL NAIL JIM DENNY POUNDED IN THAT DISAPPOINTING NIGHT?
"BOY," HE TOLD ELVIS, "YOU'D BETTER KEEP DRIVING THAT TRUCK."

Sam had been sparring with The Louisiana Hayride for several weeks over booking Elvis for its Saturday night radio program. Broadcast on KWKH, a fifty-thousand watt station in Shreveport, Louisiana, the Hayride was second only to the Grand Ole' Opry in influence with country music audiences.

In many ways, the Hayride had eclipsed the Opry in importance, especially when it came to discovering and promoting new talent. The Grand Ole' Opry was known for its stable of big-name artists, but The Louisiana Hayride made a name for itself by taking long shots on new talent—and sometimes Opry outcasts, such as Hank Williams, Jim Reeves, Kitty Wells, and Faron Young. The Opry wouldn't allow these bands to use drums, but the Hayride welcomed them. The Opry argued that it was a question of hillbilly "purity" in the music—and drums were *not* hillbilly.

Sam had decided to wait to book the Hayride until after Elvis had played the Grand Ole' Opry, for he expected a smash success in Nashville—the most prestigious booking in the whole United States.

TILLMAN FRANKS, THE NEW TALENT COORDINATOR FOR THE LOUISIANA HAYRIDE, HAD HEARD ELVIS'S RECORDING OF "THAT'S ALL RIGHT (MAMA)" ON A LOCAL SHREVEPORT RADIO SHOW. ALWAYS LOOKING FOR A NEW ACT, TILLMAN, A SLAP BASS PLAYER HIMSELF, TELEPHONED SAM AND ASKED IF HE COULD BOOK "THAT BLACK BOY WITH THE FUNNY NAME" WHO SANG THAT CATCHY NEW SONG (TILLMAN HAD NEVER SEEN ELVIS; HE'D ONLY HEARD HIS RECORDING). AT THE TIME, TILLMAN WAS "STARVIN' TO DEATH", HIS PHONE HAD BEEN TAKEN OUT OF SERVICE, AND HE MADE IT CLEAR HE WOULD JUMP AT THE CHANCE TO BOOK ELVIS FOR FIVE HUNDRED DOLLARS.

THE LOUISIANA HAYRIDE LIFTOFF

Sam replied that Elvis would be coming by the studio later that day; Sam would call Tillman back when the young man arrived and Franks could work out the details directly with Elvis. A few hours later, Tillman heard the nervous voice of Elvis say, "Mr. Franks, I heard you might be able to book me on The Louisiana Hayride."

"Yes, I think I can!" Tillman replied.

"Well, that's fine with me," Elvis answered. "We'd sure like to come down there."

D. J. Fontana, a staff drummer on the Hayride, had been given a copy of Elvis's recording to get the arrangement down. Tillman thought that D. J. needed to play drums with the trio—once more, that strange, deceptive "Sam Phillips slap-back echo" effect had struck again! Tillman got an even bigger surprise on October 16, 1954—the night Rockabilly first hit The Louisiana Hayride stage—when he discovered that Elvis Presley was not an African-American.

When showtime finally arrived, D. J. Fontana's drums sat behind a curtain, just in back of the other musicians. When Elvis, Scotty, and Bill began "That's All Right (Mama)," nothing seemed to click. The players had trouble hearing their own instruments, let alone Elvis singing. Once more, the audience reacted politely, perhaps a little shocked by the performance.

Before the second show that night, however, Tillman informed the trio that more young students would be in the audience. In his best "manager speak," Tillman also advised Elvis to "Let it all go! Get out there and give those folks a real good show." He paused, then added, "The management of the Hayride can't fire you for acting up. They haven't hired you yet!"

When Elvis and the band kicked it into high gear for the second set, the crowd began shouting and clapping . . . and Tillman knew he had a huge winner on his hands. Elvis felt the pushing accents of D. J. Fontana's drumming and wiggled and wobbled his legs and body to every beat. With each movement, the audience became more alive—clear confirmation that something very special lived in Elvis's newly generated (and gyrated) musical style.

Elvis didn't know it, but he had just opened the door very wide for many of us to follow.

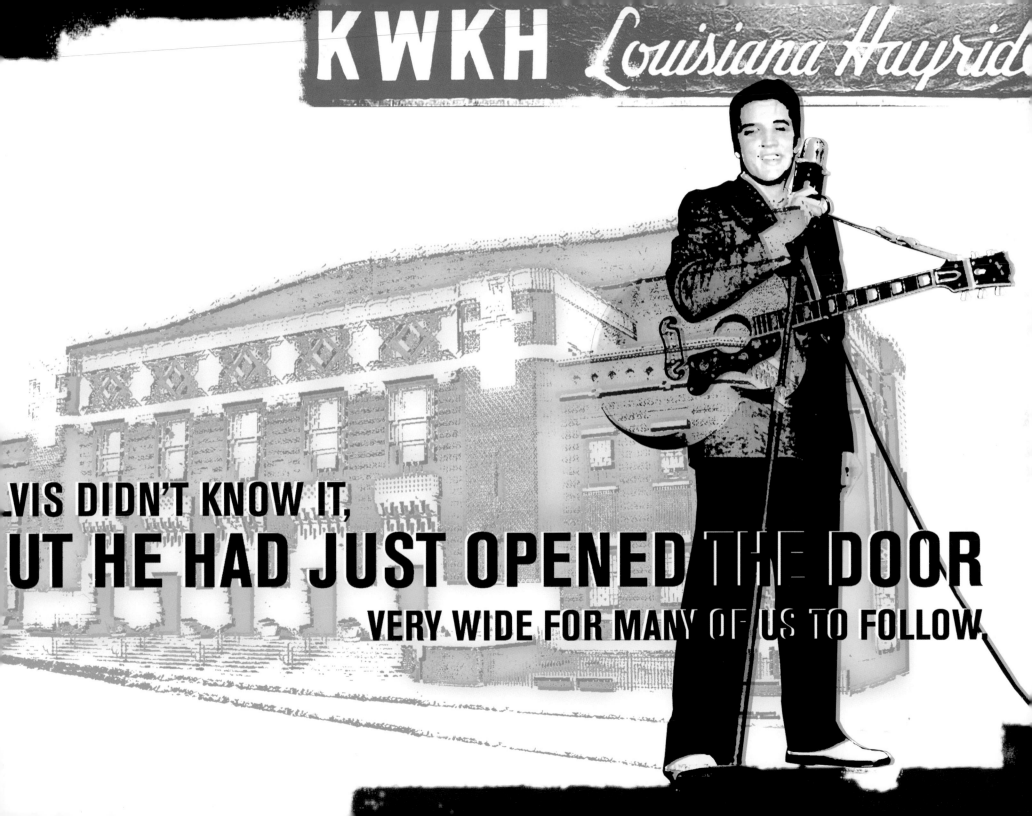

Tillman Franks: September 19, 1920 — October 26, 2006

THREE DAYS TH

T CHANGED THE WORLD

AFTER HEARING ELVIS'S NEW SOUND AND WATCHING HIM PERFORM ONSTAGE, TILLMAN FRANKS IMMEDIATELY SAW WHAT LAY AHEAD FOR THE MUSICAL WORLD. TILLMAN HOOKED HIS WAGON TO THIS STAR AND WORKED CLOSELY WITH SAM PHILLIPS AND MEMPHIS BOOKING AGENT/DISC JOCKEY BOB NEAL ON BOOKING ELVIS, SCOTTY, AND BILL THROUGHOUT MOST OF TEXAS. ONE TOUR IN PARTICULAR WOULD HAVE FAR-REACHING CONSEQUENCES FOR THE DEVELOPMENT OF ROCKABILLY.

SAN ANGELO, TEXAS: WEDNESDAY, JANUARY 5, 1955

JOE TREADWAY, DAVE STONE, AND LEROY ELMORE, WHO CO-OWNED AND MANAGED THE FULL-TIME COUNTRY MUSIC RADIO STATIONS IN SAN ANGELO AND LUBBOCK, TEXAS, OFTEN BOOKED COUNTRY MUSIC SHOWS FROM THE LOUISIANA HAYRIDE AS SPECIAL PROMOTIONS FOR KPEP, THEIR SAN ANGELO STATION, AND KDAV, IN LUBBOCK. FAMILIAR HEADLINERS SUCH AS BILLY WALKER AND THE HIT COUNTRY DUO JIMMY AND JOHNNY OFTEN TOOK THE STAGE.

Joe and his longtime friend, Tillman Franks, were always on the lookout for local talent to fill the lineup. I worked for Joe at the radio station, and he semi-managed my sprouting singing career; so for the first stop on this tour, he and Tillman Franks booked my band as the opening act. Joe also insisted that I put up all the posters for the event throughout Tom Green County, beginning a few weeks before Christmas; promote the show on my radio program; and collect tickets as patrons entered the San Angelo Civic Auditorium on the night of the performance.

The newspaper ad and playbill featured a name unfamiliar to most people: "ALVIS Presley." The spelling error, which today seems so obvious, went unnoticed until after the show. Tillman and Joe had signed Elvis, Scotty Moore, and Bill Black for five days at a total cost of one thousand dollars.

As the final ticket holders filed into their seats, I ran back to the stage door, changed my shirt, and our band—Toby Yeager, Bobby Young, Ray Deans, and I—rushed onto center stage. Our fifteen minutes went by *fast*. It seemed like a mostly uneventful performance, except for a few high school girlfriends who became a tad overzealous in their vocal support of our local recording of the first song I ever wrote, "Hillbilly Bop."

Joe smoothly managed the transition from local talent to headliner with his warm, West Texas introduction: "Friends and fans, I'd like to introduce you to a new trio of musicians from Memphis, Tennessee, and DI-RECTLY from Shreveport's Louisiana Hayride. Let's welcome to San Angelo, Texas, ALVIS PRESLEY, SCOTTY MOORE, AND BILL BLACK!" Out of respect for KPEP radio's beloved "Pappy" Joe Treadway, audience members gave polite but restrained applause to the unfamiliar act.

I positioned myself strategically backstage, as close to the action as I possibly could be while still remaining out of sight. *The only thing better than hearing Elvis Presley on record*, I thought, *has to be seeing and hearing him in person.*

Over the next fifteen minutes I experienced a sight and sound that will stay with me forever. Elvis Presley, Scotty Moore, and Bill Black worked their enticing magic in an amazing six-song performance. This was the most incredible music I'd ever heard—and here they were, performing just a few feet away from me! I stood there, spellbound. I had never known such an electrifying moment.

And clearly I wasn't alone. The initially timid audience gleefully shed its doubts and began yelling, clapping, and screaming. They kept it up throughout the entire performance.

THIS IS THE NIGHT WHEN THE ENERGETIC MAGIC OF "LIVE" ROCKABILLY MUSIC—THROUGH ELVIS, SCOTTY, AND BILL—FIRST CAPTURED MY HEART. THIS TRIO UNLEASHED THE "VIRUS." AT NEARLY EVERY PERFORMANCE ON THIS SMALL TOUR, SOME YOUNG ARTIST SHED HIS COUNTRY PERFORMANCES TO FOLLOW THE OPENING INITIATED BY ELVIS. WHAT AN EARTH-SHATTERING NIGHT FOR ME! MY WHOLE WORLD CHANGED THE FIRST TIME I WORKED WITH AND SAW ELVIS PRESLEY PERFORM. THAT NIGHT MARKED OUT MY CAREER PATH—AND I WOULDN'T BE THE ONLY ONE.

LUBBOCK, TEXAS: THURSDAY, JANUARY 6, 1955

"EVERY TIME I HEARD HIM PLAY IN SCHOOL OR AT THE USED CAR LOT OR ON TOP OF THE HI-D-HO DRIVE-IN OR IN THE SKATING RINK," SAID PEGGY SUE GERRON ABOUT BUDDY HOLLEY AND HIS BAND, "ALL THOSE YEARS, THEY WERE ALWAYS COUNTRY."

Buddy was working for KDAV, our sister station in Lubbock. Like me, Buddy had a little band that played bluegrass and country. He liked to go through the station's music library, picking records from "The Hi-D-Ho Hit Parade," then go back in the production room and listen—especially to Little Richard, Fats Domino, and any new Elvis singles. He especially liked the black artists and carefully studied this music.

Peggy Sue owned some of those records, and once when she loaned them to a friend, he intended to pass them along to Buddy. She objected. "He sings through his nose," she explained. "He's country." But that would soon change.

On Thursday, January 6, 1955, a young country and bluegrass singer named Charles Hardin "Buddy" Holley had an experience very similar to mine. As he stood backstage, watching the high-energy performance of Elvis, Scotty Moore, and Bill Black, he felt overwhelmed.

"Man, when I saw Elvis out there," Buddy later said, "I started thinking *different* about music." Buddy observed the girls screaming, out of control, to the gyrations of Elvis and declared, "That's what I want to be!"

Buddy immediately abandoned his country and bluegrass performances, picked up his Fender guitar, and began writing and singing heavy rhythm up-tempo songs greatly influenced by Elvis.

After Buddy performed on Elvis Presley's repeat show in Lubbock and had a local appearance with Bill Haley and His Comets, he captured the attention of Nashville agents and record producers. By November of 1955, Eddie Crandall, a Nashville talent agent who had heard some demo tapes cut by Holley at KDAV, notified Dave Stone, owner of the station, that Nashville record producer Owen Bradley had agreed to produce four sides of Buddy Holley for Decca Records. The recording session was scheduled for January 26, 1956, at Bradley's Barn Recording Studio in Nashville.

The session was stressful from the beginning. Bradley wouldn't allow Buddy to record with his band members, who had accompanied him to Nashville. Buddy, a very strong-willed young man, strongly voiced his displeasure. Owen Bradley had hired Nashville's best studio musicians for Buddy's session and wouldn't budge. In fact, Owen refused to allow Buddy to have any input into the production of the session.

Despite the musical disagreements, they recorded "That'll Be the Day," "Don't Come Knockin'," "Love Me," and the Sonny Curtis—written song, "Blue Days and Black Nights." Buddy felt very upset with the "sterile" arrangements and bland musical backing, and he confronted Owen Bradley about it. Buddy told Owen he would walk out of the session if he couldn't play his own guitar leads on the session and use his own band, guys who knew how he wanted the music to sound. Bradley, in turn, threatened the young and cocky singer that if he walked out, he would "never record for Decca or any other major label in Nashville" again.

Decca released the records, but with no success; and to add insult to injury, the record company misspelled Buddy's name on the label as "Holly" rather than his birth name of "Holley." (From this time on, Buddy spelled his name "Holly.") As a final insult, Decca refused to pick up Buddy's contract option and released him.

After the disappointing experience with Owen Bradley and Decca Records, Buddy concentrated on his writing and formed a new Rockabilly group with Jerry Allison on drums, Niki Sullivan on rhythm guitar, and Joe B. Maudlin slapping the upright acoustic bass. The group visited Norman Petty's studio in Clovis, New Mexico, which by then had spawned hits by Buddy Knox and Jimmy Bowen, as well as some great recordings by Buddy's close friend Roy Orbison.

Gary Tollett, a local Lubbock, Texas, performer, was preparing to record a couple of demonstration records at Petty's studio and asked his new acquaintance, Buddy Holly, to play guitar for him. Eager to record in any studio, Buddy brought along Jerry Allison and set up the demo session with Gary.

But Gary is also quick to say how they soon found out the "kids" were some of the greatest musicians they had ever heard. The Tollett's singing voices harmonized very well together, and eventually Buddy asked, "Why don't you and your wife work with me? I'm going to do some recording soon, and I'd like you to do some backup work for us."

So on the night of February 25, 1957, Buddy Holly—with Larry Welborn on bass, Jerry Allison on drums, and Niki Sullivan on acoustic guitar—visited the Norman Petty Recording Studio to record demonstration records in search of a recording contract. Gary and Ramona Tollett, along with their cousin, June Clark, gathered around the background vocals microphone with Niki Sullivan as Buddy began to sing "Looking for Someone to Love" and "That'll Be the Day." Little did anyone in the studio know that at this very moment, history was being made—history that would profoundly influence all music for generations to come.

WHEN BUDDY AND JERRY CAME STROLLING INTO THE STUDIO WEARING JEANS AND WHITE T-SHIRTS WITH THE SLEEVES ROLLED UP UNDER THEIR ARMPITS, GARY AND RAMONA TOLLETT DIDN'T THINK MUCH OF THEM. THEIR APPEARANCE AND SWAGGER GAVE OFF AN *ATTITUDE*. *WHO ARE THESE KIDS?* THEY WONDERED, ASTONISHED AT THEIR LESS-THAN-CASUAL JAMES DEAN–INSPIRED DRESS.

I'VE BEEN ASKED, "IS HE A REBEL? WAS HE A MISFIT TO THE MUSIC WORLD?" AND THE ANSWER TO BOTH QUESTIONS IS PROBABLY YES. BUDDY HOLLY WAS A REBEL IN THE SENSE THAT HE DIDN'T FOLLOW THE NORMAL TRADITIONS OF MUSIC; HE WENT OUT AND EXPLORED ON HIS OWN. LISTEN TO THE SONG, "EVERYDAY"; THAT'S JERRY ALLISON PLAYING ON HIS THIGHS. LISTEN TO A SONG LIKE "BROWN EYED HANDSOME MAN" —JERRY'S PLAYING ON A CARDBOARD BOX. HE KNEW THAT IF HE DID SOMETHING AND IT WORKED OUT BADLY, TO STOP IT AND GO ON TO SOMETHING ELSE. I RESPECT HIM FOR THAT.

— BILL GRIGGS, FIFTIES ROCK AND ROLL AND BUDDY HOLLY HISTORIAN

"Buddy was playing for an assembly and I was going out the band door at Lubbock High School and he was coming in with a guitar in hand and he knocked me over," remembers Peggy Sue Gerron. "And he ran over there and said, 'I don't have time to pick you up, but you're sure pretty.'"

Not too long afterward, Jerry Allison asked Peggy Sue for a date. "We double-dated with Buddy Holly, his best friend," Peggy remembers. "When Jerry came to the house to pick me up, Buddy and his date were sitting in the backseat. So when I got in the car, Buddy and I both started laughing. And when Jerry got in the car, he said, 'Well, what's so funny?' And Buddy said, 'Oh, I've already overwhelmed your Peggy Sue.'"

Buddy Holly and his bandmates were about to be overwhelmed themselves. Although they had no way of knowing it, their lives were about to change forever. How could Jerry and Buddy have known that their John Wayne—influenced song, "That'll Be The Day" was about to become an historic benchmark, an icon of fifties rock and roll that would skyrocket Buddy Holly and the Crickets into international stardom?

PEGGY SUE WHO?

BUDDY HOLLY HAD STARTED WRITING A SONG ABOUT A GIRL AND ASKED JERRY ALLISON TO HELP HIM FINISH IT. JERRY SUGGESTED THEY NAME THE SONG AFTER PEGGY SUE GERRON. WHY PEGGY SUE? TO FIND OUT, WE HAVE TO GO BACK A LITTLE IN TIME.

WEST TEXAS TO NEW YORK ...AND BEYOND

The Norman Petty studio version of "That'll Be the Day" just galloped along. It had absolute magic, not unlike Elvis's first accidental recording of "That's All Right (Mama)." Norman shopped the master recording, but several major labels turned it down.

Norman then got a friend of his, Bob Thiele at Brunswick Records in New York, to listen to the song without revealing the artist's name. Since Brunswick and Coral Records were subsidiaries of Decca, Norman worried about mentioning the name "Buddy Holly," remembering all too well the strong words uttered by Phil Cohen, a Decca Records executive, after the ugly incident between Holly and Owen Bradley during the Nashville sessions: "Buddy Holly—the biggest no-talent I have ever worked with!"

Bob Thiele and the other Brunswick executives liked the record and wanted to release the master, but they needed the artist's name. On the sly, Norman telephoned Jerry and Buddy in Lubbock and asked them to give him a group name for the record—and try to be quick about it. Norman felt anxious and didn't want to waste too much time on the long-distance call. Jerry and Buddy were sitting at the Allisons' kitchen table eating sandwiches. They grabbed an encyclopedia and had made it all the way to the "insects" section when Norman urged them to hurry up with the name. At that moment their fingers ran across the word *cricket*, and almost simultaneously Buddy and Jerry, laughing out loud, yelled out, "*Crickets!* How about calling us 'the Crickets'!"

And as they say, the rest is history.

Several radio stations in the East began to play the recording. A station in Buffalo, New York, played it over and over, reminiscent of the Dewey Phillips's marathon playing of "That's All Right (Mama)." By September, "That'll Be The Day" had climbed to number one on the national pop charts, setting the stage for one of the biggest Rockabilly stars of the century.

Norman Petty, in his best personal managerial voice, wrote a memo to Buddy and the Crickets with specific directives for their very first major tour. Norman's instructive memo read:

Be at the Amarillo Air Terminal Sunday evening, July 28th at least by 6:30 to check reservations and check baggage. Take enough cash along to pay for excess weight and meals between flights. Take about thirty or forty dollars cash …. the rest in Travelers Checks. Be sure to take all available identification for each member of the group. Sign only engagement contracts and nothing else. Take extra sets of guitar strings, drum sticks, heads, etc. Take out floater insurance for entire group with everyone's name on the contract. Be sure to pack records with clothes to take on trip. Take all available clean underwear …and other articles for use on trip. When you get to New York…take a cab directly to the Edison Hotel and check in there. We will meet you about noon that day. Get at least two dozen Dramamine tablets … and take one tablet at least fifteen minutes before departure. Make out trip insurance to your parents. Take at least twenty-five feet of extension cord. Take small shine kit for trip. Toilet articles of your choice. . . . Take a small Bible with you and READ IT! Be sure to get and keep receipts for all money spent. Be sure to send money to Clovis for bank account.

He signed the memo "Norman."

The tour began on August 2, 1957, at the Washington D. C. Howard Theater. On August 9 it continued on to the Royal Theatre in Baltimore, Maryland, and then moved to New York City. On August 16, the Crickets found themselves surrounded with fifties rock and roll royalty. The third concert performance took place at the legendary Apollo Theater, where the Texas lads were carefully sandwiched on the program between Danny and The Juniors ("At the Hop") and The Rays, performing their giant hit, "Daddy Cool." The Crickets were given a grand total of seven minutes to perform three songs: "That'll Be the Day," "Peggy Sue," and "Oh Boy." This amazing all-star bill also included Paul Anka, The Everly Brothers, Fats Domino, and the "Killer" himself, Jerry Lee Lewis, plus eleven other classic fifties rock and roll acts.

What a way to begin! What a night to remember! The excitement easily carried over into the next week for performances with the *Allan Freed New York City Television Show*, a packed house at the Brooklyn Paramount Theater, and then eleven straight weeks around the nation to work out the kinks with acts such as Chuck Berry, Little Richard, Jimmie Rodgers, Buddy Knox, The Drifters, and Eddie Cochran.

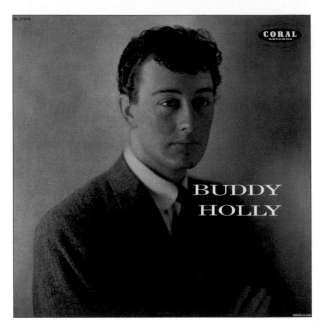

In one of the longest marathon recording sessions that Buddy Holly, Jerry Allison, Niki Sullivan, and Joe B. Maudlin would ever experience, genius spilled over and gold poured out. The session began on the night of June 29, 1957, and ended in the early morning hours of July 1. In that time Buddy Holly and The Crickets recorded "Listen to Me," "I'm Gonna Love You Too," "Oh Boy," and the debut Buddy Holly classic "Peggy Sue," dedicated to Jerry Allison's steady girlfriend, Peggy Sue Gerron. Buddy had originally written a little song with a Latin beat and named it for his niece, Cindy Lou. But as "Peggy Sue," the gentle Latin beat became enflamed rock-at-its-best, with Jerry isolated in the studio hallway, pounding the life out of his drums with "warm-up practice" paradiddles throughout the night. Buddy Holly meticulously stylized the lyric, singing and playing at a pounding pace to match Allison's wild drumming. Buddy played his Fender Stratocaster so fast that he couldn't flip the pickup switch to a different position. But since Niki Sullivan's acoustic guitar got lost in the swirl of the echo-laced loudness of Allison's drums and Holly's now legendary hypnotic guitar patterns, Niki put the rhythm guitar down and stood directly in front of Buddy in order to flip the switch on his guitar at the precise time needed to ensure Holly's seamless, rhythmic, magic instrumental lead. Moments later, as documented by record producer Norman Petty, "Peggy Sue" was born.

By October 1, 1957, "That'll Be the Day" had risen to the number one position on the national charts and was officially certified by Coral/Brunswick/ Decca Records, Inc., as having sold over one million records. It had also climbed to number one on the British music charts, as well as on those of most other countries of the world.

The week of December 9, 1957, Buddy Holly and The Crickets had three single records in the top fifty of the American national charts: "Peggy Sue," identified as a Buddy Holly solo single record, stood at the number eight position (but would soon rise to number one); "Oh Boy," by the Crickets, charted at number twenty-six; and "That'll Be the Day" enjoyed its seventeenth week on the national charts, slowly moving down from number one to number forty-three.

"That'll Be the Day" launched the Crickets to superstardom, and the group loudly celebrated with their second hit, "Oh Boy." But it was "Peggy Sue" that made Buddy Holly a household legend around the world.

BUDDY HOLLY & THE CRICKETS REPRESENT THE NEW TYPE OF RHYTHM AND SONG, & LUBBOCK, TEXAS IS CONSIDERED THE CAPITAL OF ROCKABILLY MUSIC.

— THE LUBBOCK *AVALANCHE-JOURNAL*, AUGUST 17, 1959

HOLLY AND THE CRICKETS STORM THE UK

On February 28, 1958, Buddy Holly and The Crickets, accompanied by Norman and Vi Petty, arrived in London to begin a twenty-five-day tour of the UK. Bill Haden's March 8 review of Buddy and The Crickets' performance at the famed Trocadero in London appeared in *Melody Maker* magazine under the headline, "4,500 Disc Fans Pack Troc—Despite Elvis," referring to a large crowd appearing at the Buddy Holly/Crickets concert, despite an Elvis Presley movie playing at a theater just across the street. And a smashing Birmingham, England, review read:

Buddy Holly, leader of the group, is a studious-looking young man who totes his electric guitar like a sawn-off shot-gun and carries around a giant-sized amplifier which even made the Town Hall organ pipes flinch. Mr. Holly is 70 per cent of the act. He plays and sings with brash exuberance, and adds a few Elvis Presley-like wiggles which had the teenage audience squealing with delight. The rest of the group consists of a bass player whose ability was lost in the noise and a drummer who plays with sledge-hammer precision.

Before the second show, scheduled for Hammersmith, London, Joe B. Maudlin knocked the caps off of Buddy's two front teeth during a scuffle. Buddy repaired the damage with chewing gum and performed the second show with gum spread over his broken front teeth.

Back in the Petty studio just a few days later, Buddy and Jerry Allison were joined by Tommy Allsup on lead guitar for the "It's So Easy" recording session. For some unknown reason—and surely not because of the tooth-damaging incident in England—George Atwood joined the session on bass in place of Joe B. Maudlin.

SETTING A COURSE FOR CHANGE

By mid-June of 1958, Buddy Holly flew to New York City for meetings with the record company and Peer Southern Music Publishing Company. Things were changing in the personal lives and the professional careers of the world's most successful Rockabilly band.

Buddy Holly met Maria Elena Santiago, a receptionist for a New York City music publisher, and the pair quickly made wedding plans. Buddy Holly was *always* in a hurry! Buddy and his new bride-to-be planned a double-wedding ceremony for Lubbock, Texas, along with Jerry Allison and Peggy Sue.

Buddy and The Crickets were now in great demand for the mega-tours, however, and because of stress in the group, Buddy hired studio guitarist Tommy Allsup to come along on the summer tour schedule in an effort to generate a more professional stability, onstage and off. Holly also thought that he and the Crickets should produce their own records and wanted to break their professional relationship with Norman Petty.

But despite Buddy's plans for the double wedding, Jerry and Peggy Sue jumped the gun and eloped instead. They got married in Honey Grove, Texas, on July 22, 1958. Shocked by this development, Buddy telephoned Peggy Sue from New York City and asked, "Did you really marry that drummer Jerry Allison?"

On August 15, 1958, Charles Hardin "Buddy" Holley and Maria Elena Santiago were married at the home of his parents, L. O. and Ella Holley, in Lubbock, Texas. Buddy's brothers, Larry and Travis, and his sister, Patricia, took part in the ceremony. The newly wed Jerry and Peggy Sue Allison also attended the small gathering. And then the Holleys and the Allisons flew to Acapulco, Mexico, for a two-week honeymoon. For the fall tours of 1958, again Buddy insisted that Tommy Allsup accompany the group on lead guitar. He also hired The Roses—Robert Linville and David Bigham—for background vocal group support.

Immediately after the tour, Buddy decided to leave the Crickets and Norman Petty behind, so on November 3, 1958, he terminated his business relationship with Petty and moved to New York City. Peggy Sue remembers how the tears flowed from everyone because of this separation. Stunned by the breakup of the group, Tommy Allsup emphatically stated, "Without Buddy Holly, there is no Crickets." One could also hardly ignore the prophetic words of the British press just months earlier, which emphatically stated, "Mr. Holly is 70 per cent of the act."

On a small Ampex tape recorder in his Greenwich Village apartment, Buddy recorded several new songs he had written. In a letter to his parents, Buddy wrote, "I've been writing a few songs. The best one to date is a 'top secret' one titled "Peggy Sue Got Married." Please don't mention it to anyone. I want this to be a surprise."

WHERE DO WE GO WHEN THE SHOW CLOSES?

Without his friends, Jerry and Joe B., Buddy had to make some serious decisions about who would back him on the Winter Dance Party tour throughout the midwestern United States. He recruited his stable studio musician companion, Tommy Allsup, to play lead guitar, along with Lubbock disc jockey friend Waylon Jennings on bass, with Carl Bunch on drums. After a few days of rehearsal in Buddy's Greenwich Village apartment, the four boarded a train to meet up with J. P. "The Big Bopper"

The tour kicked off in Milwaukee, Wisconsin, but rapidly stalled out when the band's tour bus broke down in the thirty-below-zero temperatures. Buddy and the other performers burned newspapers in the aisle of the bus to try to keep warm. With assistance from the local sheriff's department, the entertainers got rescued, but Carl Bunch had to be hospitalized with frostbite.

On February 2, 1959, Buddy Holly, Tommy Allsup, and Waylon Jennings performed and served as the backup group for the other entertainers at the Surf Ballroom in Clear Lake, Iowa. When the show ended, Buddy Holly, Ritchie Valens, and The Big Bopper boarded a small single engine chartered private airplane. Shortly after takeoff, the plane crashed in a nearby cornfield, killing all on board.

EIGHTEEN LIGHTNING-FAST MONTHS INTO HIS BRILLIANT CAREER, BUDDY HOLLY DIED AT THE AGE OF TWENTY-TWO, LEAVING A LEGACY OF UNIQUE CREATIVE INFLUENCE. THE GREATEST OF THE GREATS IN THE ENTERTAINMENT INDUSTRY—JOHN LENNON, PAUL MCCARTNEY, ELTON JOHN, THE ROLLING STONES, ERIC CLAPTON, BRUCE SPRINGSTEEN, BOB DYLAN, KRIS KRISTOFFERSON, AND MANY OTHERS—READILY ADMITTED TO HOLLY'S SPECTACULAR INFLUENCE ON THEIR OWN CAREERS AND MUSIC.

"I was driving home from lunch in my father's white '57 Ford on the morning of February 3, 1959," remembers Bill Griggs, "and as we kids did, we had on the radio. I didn't like what was playing. I remember turning the dial and finding WPOP in Hartford, Connecticut. They're playing 'That'll Be the Day'—always my favorite song, Buddy Holly and The Crickets—and I cranked that sucker up. And I'm sitting there, keeping the beat on the dashboard, as we did. When the song ended, the DJ said, 'And that is yet another song by the late Buddy Holly, who died this morning in a plane crash.'

"I remember pulling to the side of the road. There's no tears. It was shock and I've said many times since, 'You know, our heroes aren't supposed to die—but one just did.'"

"I thought the world had come to an end when Buddy died," agreed David Bigham. "We had just toured with Buddy in the fall of '58, and of course he died February 3, 1959. And we had big dreams. The Roses had big dreams and our leader, our hero, our inspiration, had passed on."

Buddy's own parents heard about the tragedy from Lubbock disc jockey Bill Mack as he read a KDAV Radio news bulletin. Mack, a friend and next door neighbor of the Holleys, was sure the proper authorities had notified the family before he received the news wire bulletin. But they hadn't, and he still suffers for this sad turn of events.

A PERSONAL REFLECTION

It is a vast understatement to say that Buddy Holly and The Crickets were one of the most influential Rockabilly acts of the twentieth century. Some thought of Buddy as shy and withdrawn, perhaps a bit of a nerd, but his legendary talents completely overpowered any such image.

The day Buddy Holly died, I was working as a disc jockey at KHEY Radio in El Paso, Texas, and in the evenings performing across the border in Juarez at the La Fiesta Supper Club. I was alone in the studio that morning when I heard the warning bell of the United Press International teletype begin to signal an "urgent" news break. I strolled over to read the headline: "Buddy Holly, Ritchie Valens and 'The Big Bopper' killed in a plane crash in Mason City, Iowa." I didn't read on, because I couldn't. I couldn't get my breath.

I panicked because the record spinning on the radio turntable was nearly over and I knew I had to read some commercials and introduce the next recording. I also knew that I could not speak; my throat felt paralyzed. I was panic-stricken. The worst thing that can happen to a radio announcer is to turn on your microphone, open your mouth to speak . . . and have nothing come out.

Just a day before, I had visited with Don Guess, a musician who had worked with Buddy Holly in Lubbock during Buddy's country music days. I had brushed by Buddy once or twice at KDAV back in 1955. Of course, I was acutely aware of his fledgling career from the very early days, as well as the Crickets' 1957-58 mega-success.

The record ended and I switched open the mic. Just as I did, however, I began to cry. With my voice trembling, I read aloud the headline of the UPI news article and continued to read, robotically, the entire story. I had no idea what I was saying.

As I finished, the door to the control room softly opened, and my friend, radio station program director and fellow announcer Mike Oatman, walked in. His face revealed that he also had heard the news. He saw I was not doing well and began to talk with me, live on the radio.

"Tell me about the first time you met Buddy," he said. "Didn't you both work for Dave Stone's stations, KDAV in Lubbock and KPEP in San Angelo?"

I don't remember answering him, but I suppose I did. I have no recollection of what I said.

Many times I have been asked what it was like to become the lead singer of the Crickets after the death of Buddy Holly. Well, first I had to deal with the horror of Buddy's death, as did millions of others around the world. The most difficult time I had in coping with Buddy's death, however, occurred when I first joined the Crickets.

Jerry Allison and I arrived at United Recording
Studio in Los Angeles to record a new album with
Bobby Vee, already in production. Here I was,
the new lead singer of the Crickets—but that was
Buddy's place, *his* job, the position *he* created with *his*
unique talent and singing style. Even though some
said they heard similarities between his singing
and mine, I couldn't fathom the comparison. My
new acquaintance and soon to be lifelong friend
Bobby Vee helped me very much, and somehow we
got through the sessions. Fortunately, the album
Bobby Vee Meets The Crickets became a huge hit inter-
nationally. But the fear never left me each time
we performed or recorded—the fear that someone
would say, "What are you doing, building a career
on Buddy Holly's grave?" Fortunately, no one ever
said such a thing to me. And I have no idea how I
would have reacted if they had.

THE WORLD WILL NEVER KNOW WHAT BUDDY HOLLY WOULD HAVE TURNED INTO. THERE'S NO TELLING WHERE HE WOULD HAVE GONE, NO TELLING HOW PROGRESSIVE HE WOULD HAVE GOTTEN. BUDDY HOLLY WAS A GREAT LOSS.

– CHARLIE DANIELS

I have only one major disappointment in my life regarding Buddy Holly—I wish I had known him more personally. I knew Buddy only through his amazing creative works and through those who knew him personally.

I have often spoken about Buddy with his Crickets bandmate, co-writer, friend, and drummer, Jerry Ivan Allison. I've had similar conversations with Sonny Curtis, the soft-spoken creative genius who was also Buddy's fellow musician and friend. And I have gotten better acquainted with Buddy over the decades through one of my dearest friends, Peggy Sue Gerron, Buddy's real-life "Peggy Sue," who loved Buddy deeply (and was loved in return).

Robert Linville and David Bigham, who made up The Roses performing group that recorded background vocals and toured with Holly and the Crickets, also have shared insights of their close relationship with Buddy—in the process warming my heart and giving me a broader insight into the real Buddy Holly. My good friend Tommy Allsup has honestly and bluntly spoken of his close relationship with Buddy, yet in a most genteel, respectful way. I have grown greatly from Tommy's recollections.

ONLY ONE DISAPPOINTMENT

And Maria Elena, Buddy's widow, has nourished my hunger to get closer to Buddy, particularly as the result of an extensive and memorable time we shared in Sedona, Arizona, in 1999. I'm pleased that some of this exchange was videotaped for posterity. It strengthens me to revisit this intimate interview-conversation I had with Maria about her deceased husband, especially the flashback of Maria and I standing side by side at center stage and singing "Raining in My Heart" as a special tribute to Buddy. This experience has continued to exert something of a spiritual influence on me.

In so many ways, I have come to know Buddy Holly intimately. Without question, my life has been heavily influenced by everything he did professionally. Buddy Holly posthumously passed on so many gifts to me, for which I feel constantly humbled and forever thankful.

ONE THING I KNOW FOR SURE: BUDDY HOLLY REMAINS A UNIQUE ENTERTAINMENT ICON, A VERY SPECIAL ARTIST WITH EXTRAORDINARY TALENT AS A SONGWRITER, GUITARIST, AND VOCAL STYLIST. NO ONE COULD EVER REPLACE HIM. AS ONE OF THE MOST INFLUENTIAL ENTERTAINERS OF THE TWENTIETH CENTURY, BUDDY HOLLY'S MUSIC IS TRULY IMMORTAL.

MOSTLY, BUDDY PLAYED THAT FENDER STRATOCASTER WRONG. MOST GUITARISTS PLAY IT DOWN,
UP, DOWN UP. BUDDY PLAYED ALL DOWN STROKES. SO HE'S HITTING THE BASS CHORD OF THAT
GUITAR FIRST. NOW IT'S CALLED RHYTHM LEAD, AND IT MAKES A VERY UNIQUE SOUND.
IF YOU WANT TO PLAY LIKE BUDDY HOLLY, YOU HAVE TO PLAY THE GUITAR WRONG TO MAKE IT RIGHT.

– BILL GRIGGS, FIFTIES ROCK AND ROLL AND BUDDY HOLLY HISTORIAN

THE HOLLY FACTOR

Despite his early death, Buddy Holly became a huge influence on the musicians who followed him. You can hardly talk about a kid picking up a Fender Stratocaster and playing music in his garage without acknowledging Buddy Holly's role. Few twentieth-century entertainers impacted the world of music as greatly as he did.

Before Buddy Holly and The Crickets, nobody wore glasses onstage. His influence touched many superstars, including The Beatles. In fact, The Beatles named themselves after the Crickets, had the same basic lineup as the Crickets, and all their early songs were American rock and roll. The very first song the young Beatles (or Quarrymen, as they were known then) recorded on a cheap acetate disc

When I asked Kris Kristofferson how Buddy Holly most impressed him, he thoughtfully stated, "I liked the way he grew so fast. Well, I guess he didn't have time to do anything else. I was so surprised when you said he died eighteen months after his first hit. Yeah, I just can't help but think of what a wonderful writer he would have been if he'd lived a little bit longer. I would have loved to see what he was writing when he was my age now. I've often thought back when I wrote 'Me and Bobby McGee'— I thought, *Buddy Holly could have written this.*"

How greatly the music world would have been deprived if Charles Hardin "Buddy" Holley had never seen Elvis Presley perform on that Thursday night of the magical, Tillman Franks/Joe Treadway—promoted "Three Nights in West Texas Tour"! While I'm glad we'll never know such deprivation, we do know what happened the last night of the tour, when the Elvis phenomenon moved to yet a third West Texas town.

Charles Hardin Holley: September 7, 1936 — February 3, 1959

MIDLAND, TEXAS: FRIDAY, JANUARY 7, 1955

AFTER LUBBOCK, THE NEXT LOUISIANA HAYRIDE "ELVIS PRESLEY ROAD SHOW" EXPLOSION HIT MIDLAND, TEXAS. AND THIS WOULD BE ROY ORBISON'S TURN FOR A MUSICAL REVELATION. MUSIC HAD INTRIGUED ROY SINCE AT LEAST AGE SIX, WHEN HE ASKED HIS DAD FOR A HARMONICA BUT GOT A GUITAR.

How can one explain what it felt like to live within the close confines of this West Texas triangle of historic musical change? I grew up within a hundred miles of Roy. Our ragtag groups played dates together when it was just Roy Orbison and the Wink Westerners—a group he founded in 1949, at age thirteen—and later when it was Roy Orbison and the Teen Kings. At that time, Roy was doing his little country things and struggling to unleash whatever greatness was going to happen for him.

Hank Williams's blues-edged singing style and the depth of Hank's writing heavily influenced Roy Orbison. At ten years of age, Roy was singing the Hank Williams classics "Lovesick Blues" and "Kaw-liga"—and being recognized for it. In 1946 a medicine show came to Vernon, Texas. Roy entered the talent contest, belted out a Hank Williams song, and tied for first place with a fifteen-year-old kid. The total prize came to fifteen dollars, so Orbison won $7.50 and gave his buddy half of it for carrying his guitar. That's a true *Orbisonism* trait that stayed with him his whole life.

Many people thought Roy Orbison's thick glasses were a sign of flawed vision, but with the Elvis experience, Roy could suddenly see very clearly—and was about to realize his greatest vision.

On the third night of the Elvis tour, Roy saw his world flip upside down. He watched dumbfounded as Elvis gave an electrifying performance, complete with wild, gyrating antics. Just as Buddy Holly and I before him, Roy immediately discarded his hillbilly career, picked up his guitar and focused on a funny little Rockabilly song cowritten by two North Texas State College friends, Lee Moore and Dick Penner, oddly titled "Ooby Dooby."

In December of 1955, Roy traveled to Dallas, Texas, and recorded "Ooby Dooby," supposedly for Columbia records. It turned out that Roy and his pals were taken in, some even say used. The producer wanted Roy to sing the song only as a demo for another performer. He never intended that Roy's version become a single record.

Roy remembers, "The next thing we heard was from our local record store owner, 'Papa' (Cecil) Hollifield, who said 'Ooby Dooby' was coming out by a group called Sid King and the Five Strings, on Columbia Records."

ROY ORBISON IS ANOTHER WEST TEXAN. HE'S FROM WINK, TEXAS. I'LL PUT WEST TEXAS UP AGAINST ANY PART OF THE WORLD, AS FAR AS THE AMOUNT OF SINGERS, SONGWRITERS, AND MUSICIANS THAT WE'VE PRODUCED.

– BILL GRIGGS, FIFTIES ROCK AND ROLL/ROCKABILLY HISTORIAN

On Saturday nights, Roy and the Teen Kings regularly played the Saturday Night Jamboree in Jal, New Mexico. Taking their cues from Elvis, Scotty Moore, and Bill Black, Roy and the Teen Kings added songs like "That's All Right (Mama)," "Rock Around the Clock," and "Ooby Dooby" to their repertoire and were well received for their new Rockabilly sound.

Local West Texas promoters Weldon Rogers and C. C. Oliver approached Roy about recording for their newly formed Je-Wel Records label. Norman Petty and his wife, Vi, formed two-thirds of the Norman Petty Trio. The trio's pop records had become very well known nationally, and Norman's home studio in Clovis, New Mexico, was used solely for their recordings; it had not yet become available as a commercial recording facility. When Roy heard that Norman Petty had some recording gear, however, he literally drove over to New Mexico, knocked on Petty's door, and said, "I'm Roy Orbison from Wink, Texas, and I want to record this song 'Ooby Dooby.'" Norman felt a bit taken back by Roy, but looked him over and then said, with no further questions, "Okay, come on in." And that day Roy and the Teen Kings recorded a great version of "Ooby Dooby"—in fact, my personal favorite. Two weeks later, on March 19, 1956, the record was released on Je-Wel Records.

Looking for a legitimate recording opportunity, Roy approached Johnny Cash—the two of them had met while performing on The Louisiana Hayride shows in West Texas—and asked him, "Where should I record? Do you think you could get me in with Sam Phillips?" Johnny handed him the telephone number and said, "Call him."

Roy called Sam in his very gentlemanly and soft-spoken way—and Sam yelled back, "I don't need any more singers! I've got all I need, and Johnny Cash doesn't run my record company!" While Roy stood on the Texas end of this long-distance telephone conversation, absolutely stunned, Sam Phillips abruptly hung up the phone.

Roy rushed the recording over to the record store of his friend Papa Hollifield in nearby Odessa, Texas, and Papa loved it. Hollifield believed this second version of "Ooby Dooby" had that rare, spontaneous magic so evident in Elvis Presley's Rockabilly songs, and immediately he telephoned Sam Phillips at Sun Records in Memphis. Hollifield played "Ooby Dooby" on the telephone for Phillips, and the man who just a few months before had so angrily hung up on Roy Orbison, anxiously responded to Hollifield and Orbison, "Can you be down here in three days?" And there, at Sun Records, Roy Orbison and the Teen Kings recorded "Ooby Dooby" for the third time.

SAM SIGNED ROY TO AN EXCLUSIVE RECORDING CONTRACT IN 1956, FORGETTING ALL ABOUT
HIS EARLIER RUDE BRUSH-OFF. ROY'S PERSISTENCE AND TALENT CARRIED HIM INTO SAM'S STABLE
AND RIGHT UP THE NATIONAL CHARTS WITH "OOBY DOOBY." THIS THIRD VERSION OF THE SONG
SCALED THE BOTTOM RUNGS TO REACH THE NUMBER FIFTY-NINE POSITION OF THE NATIONAL
BILLBOARD MAGAZINE CHARTS IN JUNE 1956. SO ALTHOUGH THE FUSE WAS LIT, THIS WEST TEXAS
ROCKET HADN'T YET MADE IT TO THE MOON.

ROY CALLED SAM IN HIS VERY GENTLEMANLY AND QUIET SPOKEN WAY— AND SAM YELLED BACK, "I DON'T NEED MORE SINGERS. I'VE GOT ALL I NEED, AND JOHNNY CASH DOESN'T RUN MY RECORD COMPANY."

ELVIS PRESLEY WAS ONCE ASKED, "WHO DO YOU FEAR?" ELVIS NEVER ANSWERED THAT QUESTION, BUT HE SAID, "I THINK THE GREATEST VOICE IN THE WORLD IS ROY ORBISON."

– BILL GRIGGS, FIFTIES ROCK AND ROLL/ROCKABILLY HISTORIAN

While "Ooby Dooby" became an international Rockabilly classic, in fact it was only what is commonly called a "radio turntable" hit. Even though it climbed its way to the midposition of the national music charts, Sam Phillips felt overcome with his oversized debts at Sun Records and just couldn't afford to properly promote the single record nationally as it should have been.

But Roy Orbison had caught the Rockabilly fever and quickly went on to record some other remarkable fifties rock and roll/Rockabilly classics at Sun, including the memorable "Rockhouse" and "A Cat Called Domino." Roy *felt* the music. That's all he wanted to do—play and sing this new rhythm and rock music. He knew he was on the threshold of something great, but just didn't know if Sam Phillips and his Sun Records were going to sink in a load of debt or ride the curl of the waves to Rockabilly success.

In this interim time the Teen Kings became discouraged, packed up their gear, and moved back to West Texas. Feeling like he was stuck in the middle of a Memphis swamp, a saddened Roy Orbison struggled to overcome his disappointment in Sam by fine-tuning his songwriting skills.

Much like the 1956 Elvis Presley situation, everything at Sun Records was always for sale at the right price. So in 1958, Sam Phillips readily accepted the sale of Roy's recording contract to RCA Records and Acuff-Rose Music Publishing Company in Nashville, Tennessee.

By focusing on his songwriting, Roy found early success with a song he wrote and dedicated to his longtime Lubbock, Texas, girlfriend, "Claudette." In March of 1958, Roy played a show in Hammond, Indiana, with The Everly Brothers, who were looking for a song to record for their next single record session. When Roy sang his "Claudette" for them, Don and Phil excitedly asked him to write the lyrics down on a shoe box top—the only paper they could find. Cadence Records recorded "Claudette" and "All I Have to Do Is Dream" with The Everly Brothers on my nineteenth birthday, March 6, 1958, and "All I Have to Do Is Dream" became their third number one, million-selling single record, staying on top of the national charts for five weeks. Roy Orbison's "Claudette," the B-side of the recording, rose to number thirty on the national *Billboard* magazine pop charts and marked Roy as a writer-singer-performer. Wesley Rose, co-owner of Acuff-Rose Music Publishing Company, quickly got Roy a new recording contract with the newly formed and independent Monument Records, owned by Fred Foster.

Not long ago, Fred reminisced with me about his first meetings with Roy: "When Wesley Rose asked if I had heard of Roy Orbison, I said, 'If he's the guy who did "Ooby Dooby" and "Rock House," I have.'" When Roy moved back to Texas, he teamed up with writing partner Joe Melson and the duo began a successful collaboration that launched Roy Orbison, the entertainer, to superstardom.

When in 1985 Roy began discussing Fred Foster and Monument Records with my friend and partner, Red Robinson, Roy recollected, "I started recording for Fred Foster and Monument Records, and so I remember driving from Texas to Memphis and then on to Nashville. And I was prepared to fight for strings. I wanted to use strings on the record and voices and orchestral arrangements and stuff—you know, real good things like real musicians, because I didn't have any of that support at Sun."

Fred Foster rarely gives interviews, and talking to him was like having a family reunion with the closest associate of a dear friend. Fred emotionally recalled those wonderful days when Roy brought the beginning of his greatness to the Monument studios. He freely gave me a much-appreciated music history lesson with the cadence of an Oxford professor: "Music was going through a revolution, or an evolution, and nobody was really experienced in the new music, so to speak. I didn't know what I was doing. So, what I was reduced to doing—which I think would work very well today, or anytime—was doing what I liked. What you could feel!"

He then added a helpful lesson from his basic music philosophy: "Maybe I am odd, but I'm not totally odd. I mean, there must be a million odd people in America like me. So, if I loved something, there's a million others at least that are gonna love it. It could be many millions, you know. So, my motto was, 'Stay true to the music and make it as good as you can make it!'"

Roy painted a poignant picture of this remarkable recording partnership when he said, "'Running Scared' was the first big ballad, and that's full voice. It was falsetto at the end of the record for the first two or three takes we ran through. However, Fred came over the intercom thing and he embarrassed me. He said, 'Roy, you're gonna lose this record if you don't sing out more on the last note.'"

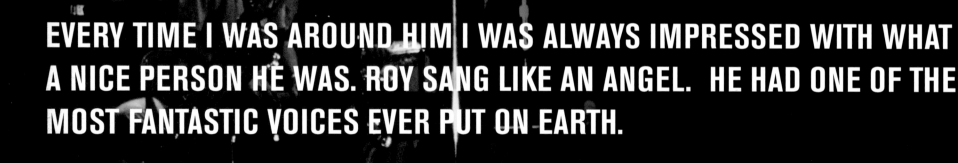

EVERY TIME I WAS AROUND HIM I WAS ALWAYS IMPRESSED WITH WHAT A NICE PERSON HE WAS. ROY SANG LIKE AN ANGEL. HE HAD ONE OF THE MOST FANTASTIC VOICES EVER PUT ON EARTH.

— KRIS KRISTOFFERSON, SONGWRITER, SINGER AND ACTOR

Monument
45-447

Crying

ROY ORBISON sings...

Candy Man

with BOB MOORE'S orchestra and chorus

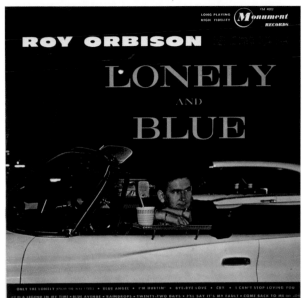

In telling his version of the story to me, Fred said, "When Roy got down to the high note, he hit it full voice—absolutely perfectly."

Roy Orbison's 1960 hit "Only the Lonely" made him an international star, even though Elvis kept it out of the number one position; it peaked at number two on the *Billboard* charts. Roy did corner the market on "number one" on the British charts, however. His subsequent hit, the big-ending "Running Scared," was Roy's debut number one nationally-charted recording in the United States. In our Rockabilly documentary interview, Roy told my co-host, Red Robinson, exactly what that felt like: "By the time I got to 'Running Scared,' with Fred Foster as my friend and record producer, it was a special freedom and growth—and I was wide open. I could do anything I wanted to, which was great for an artist at that time."

Fred Foster stimulated Roy's fifties rock and roll/Rockabilly creativity by introducing him to the classical side of things with Ravel's "Bolero." Fred especially wanted Roy to experience the rhythm and timing of the classical composition.

Several contributing factors helped Roy to achieve his enormous success. His songs were completely original, the performances were unique, and the production was free-flowing. Fred Foster consistently opted for quality rather than quantity and was always willing to take a chance on something new and different—if it felt good to him.

This process generated amazing hits for Roy Orbison: "Crying," "Candy Man," "Dream Baby," "Working for the Man," "Leah," "In Dreams," "Pretty Paper," "Blue Bayou," "Mean Woman Blues," and "It's Over"—a string of hits that lasted for more than four years. Roy Orbision became the top-selling American artist and one of the world's biggest names in entertainment.

In May of 1963, Roy headlined a British tour with the hot new group, The Beatles, who meant nothing to most music fans in the United States at that time. The entire tour sold out in a single afternoon, and on the first night, Roy did fourteen encores before The Beatles could even get onstage to perform—a remarkable and long journey away from that memorable night on January 7, 1955, in West Texas.

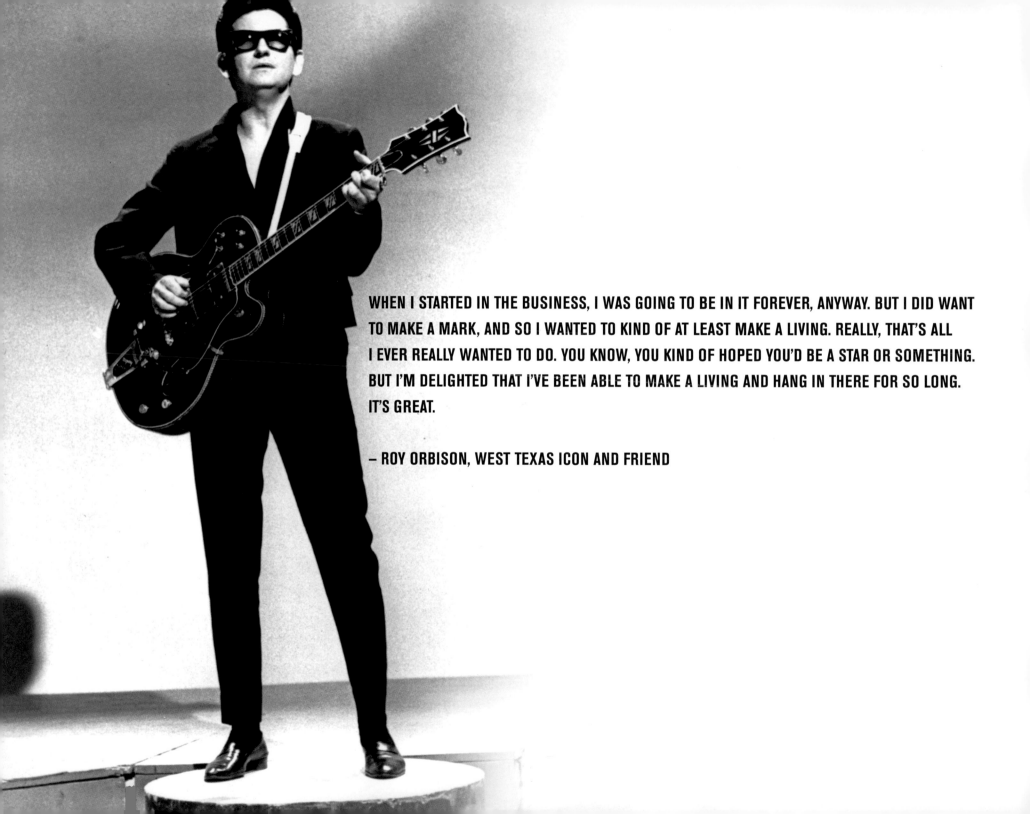

WHEN I STARTED IN THE BUSINESS, I WAS GOING TO BE IN IT FOREVER, ANYWAY. BUT I DID WANT
TO MAKE A MARK, AND SO I WANTED TO KIND OF AT LEAST MAKE A LIVING. REALLY, THAT'S ALL
I EVER REALLY WANTED TO DO. YOU KNOW, YOU KIND OF HOPED YOU'D BE A STAR OR SOMETHING.
BUT I'M DELIGHTED THAT I'VE BEEN ABLE TO MAKE A LIVING AND HANG IN THERE FOR SO LONG.
IT'S GREAT.

– ROY ORBISON, WEST TEXAS ICON AND FRIEND

Roy recorded "Oh Pretty Woman" on August 1, 1964, at the peak of the so-called British Invasion. He cowrote this stellar anthem with his new writing partner, Bill Dees. It soon became Roy Orbison's biggest hit and, in fact, one of the world's best-known songs of all time. Roy carefully digested Fred Foster's sage advice, put all of it into practice, and with this ruby anthem indeed made his ascension onto the worldwide pinnacle of music history. This classic Roy Orbison work became his signature song. "Oh Pretty Woman" vaulted to the number one position on all the national charts in virtually every country in the world and sold over seven million copies in its first year of release.

From the very peak of the summit, any fall must have been unthinkable. Yet a scant two years later, Roy fell from this amazing height to a staggering low when his wife, Claudette, was killed in a motorcycle accident while they were riding near their home in Hendersonville, Tennessee. And just as he was beginning to heal from this great loss, only two years later tragedy struck again while Roy was on tour in Australia: Two of his three children died when his Hendersonville home burned to the ground.

Only God knows the measure of strength it takes to resolve this kind of pain and loss. Yet somehow Roy picked himself up, dug deep into his soul, gathered God's strength, and continued on along his inimitable track.

Bob Dylan spoke for many in his autobiography when he wrote of Roy Orbison, "There wasn't anything else on the radio like him. I'd listen and wait for another song, but next to Roy, the playlist was strictly dullsville . . . gutless and flabby."

Roy was inducted into the Rock and Roll Hall of Fame and Museum in 1987, along with Carl Perkins, and in 1998 he posthumously received the Recording Academy's Lifetime Achievement Award.

On January 18, 1978, Roy had heart surgery at St. Thomas Hospital in Nashville, Tennessee. But not even the greatest heart surgeons in the world could extract Roy's layers of pain and suffering for the massive loss of his wife, Claudette, whom he'd married in 1957, plus his precious two children, whom he'd lost by fire in 1968. And so Roy's heart gave up the fight on December 6, 1988. He was fifty-two years old.

On that very morning, my wife, Pamela, and I casually walked out of the Laura Ashley Shop at 451 Oxford Street, Marble Arch, London. The newspaper headline struck me with gale force as I read, "Roy Orbison Dead from a Heart Attack at 52." The sidewalk slapped me on the knees and I remembered and I cried.

There's only one Roy Orbison! Just imagine the musical and lyrical stretch from "Ooby Dooby" to "Oh Pretty Woman"—for any normal human being, that would be totally unrealistic.

And yet a single Friday night in Midland, Texas, gave flight to Roy Orbison's changed course of life. What he saw and heard on January 7, 1955, startled him onto the road to Rockabilly and fifties rock and roll.

"We were pioneers and all," Roy explained, "but we were also caught up in it. It was brand new for us, just like it was for everybody else—and really exciting. Rockabilly, it was the only music we wanted to make."

ROY ORBISON MAY HAVE STUDIED FOR A DEGREE IN GEOLOGY, BUT HE MINED A DOCTORATE IN ROCK!

Roy Kelton Orbison: April 23, 1936 — December 6, 1988

THE LIST GOES ON

Those three nights—January 5, 6, and 7, 1955—literally changed the music world forever. The Beatles trace their inspiration to that famous Louisiana Hayride tour, as can countless other acts that followed, from Buddy Holly and The Crickets to Roy Orbison to Waylon Jennings. The list grows longer even today.

Three amazing nights in West Texas so many decades ago prompted enormous changes in American music, affecting the lives of millions around the world—and especially the lives of young singer-performers like us who yearned for a music magically rooted in Southern gospel, black blues, African-American spirituals, bluegrass, and hillbilly.

We called it Rockabilly long before anyone else called it rock and roll!

All of us who helped to pioneer Rockabilly shared a major common denominator. Each of us was born into a modest, rural farming family; each had a strong Christian mother who helped form our foundational beliefs through continual prayer; and each regularly attended and sang in our local churches, beginning at a very early age. In fact, the roots of Rockabilly sink deep into the "Precious Memories" of Southern gospel music in the rural churches of Arkansas, Tennessee, Virginia, Texas, and Louisiana.

And we find one of the best examples of this strong Christian foundation in the amazing man with the "Blue Suede Shoes" —Carl Perkins, from Tiptonville, Tennessee.

IT'S IN THE SOUL

In a 1995 interview, the man known around the world as "the Godfather of Rockabilly," the legendary Carl Perkins, spoke boldly about both his music and his church.

"Southern gospel music means everything to me," he declared. "I can't tell you every word the preacher said on Sunday morning, but the old church gospel music was part of me from birth. It had a lot of influence on my entire career. My mama always saw to it that we went to church. I can remember from age six, seven, and eight, on up through those years, the preacher telling us about this beautiful name of Jesus. It had such a beautiful ring to it. I thought, *That's the greatest name I've ever heard. What a name!"*

Carl got really energized when he recalled those early days, growing up in a small, rural church. And even back then, he had begun to develop a sense of the kind of music he could call his own:

When they sang "Amazing Grace" in the slow, dragging feel, that didn't move me much. It's very pretty, but when they would hit, "Some glad morning, when this life is o'er, I'll fly away," that old shoe of little Carl Lee Perkins would be hitting the raw plank floor of that Baptist church, knocking up dust. Mama would reach over and capture my big ear between her strong fingers, pull me close to her face, and admonish, "Carl Lee, you're singing too loud, your foot's slapping the floor too hard, and you're wiggling too much." But I couldn't help it. Albert Brumley's "I'll Fly Away" was taking me for a ride. It had a feel to it. The up-tempo, moving gospel music got under my skin and burrowed into my soul. It influenced the way I played music forever, and it shaped the kind of music I wrote and recorded. I love Southern gospel. It's a major part of our Rockabilly.

From the very earliest time in his life, music lifted Carl's soul and helped him connect with the deepest part of the human experience. "Music is freedom," he told me. "And Rockabilly music is happy music. There's nothing better than being free and happy. That's what we all need more of."

Carl Perkins was born the son of Lake County, Tennessee, sharecroppers. And on this earthy foundation, six-year-old Carl began his formal musical education.

As he worked the cotton fields, Carl experienced the first stirrings of music's power to move his heart. The rhythmic, spiritual music of his black coworkers planted seeds deep in his soul that would germinate, blossom, and grow in years to come.

Gripped by the black gospel sound of the cotton row melodies, Carl took an early interest in his father's Saturday night ritual of listening to the Grand Ole' Opry. His daddy's battery powered radio afforded him the luxury of absorbing Jimmie Rodgers' fusion of blues, pop, and country music. From the hills of Virginia came the Carter Family, who transformed commercial country music into their own graceful, haunting harmonies and vocal solos. Roy Acuff, the undisputed king of country music, brought lyrics from the Old Testament into the Perkins' radio on the wings of "The Great Speckled Bird." Acuff inspired Carl to ask his parents for a guitar of his own. Bill Monroe's band, the Bluegrass Boys, shook up Carl and country music with its spirited tempos, breakneck mandolin solos, and Bill's often screeching, high-pitched vocal performances.

THIS WAS "MUSIC 101" FOR AN EAGER YOUNG CARL PERKINS

THE SON OF SHARECROPPERS

At this early age, Carl learned to play the guitar from an old black friend he called "Uncle John." Uncle John Westbrook placed his long, bony fingers on top of Carl's small hands and helped him form the chords on the guitar neck. Uncle John also gave Carl his most valuable counsel: "See, Carl Lee, it ain't just in the guitar; it's in the fingers. What I mean by that is—it's in the soul."

When the six-year old Carl Lee Perkins challenged his mentor as to how he could get that "soul" into his fingers, Uncle John motioned for him to lean his head down on the guitar. "Get down close to it. You can feel the music travel from the strangs, up through your head, and down to your soul where you live. You can feel it. Let it *vi-ber-ate*." These wise words would one day elevate Carl Perkins to superstardom and raise him up to be the godfather of Rockabilly.

ELVIS STRIKES AGAIN

Carl Perkins and his two brothers, Jay and Clayton, played all the area honky-tonks and gained a strong following with their innovative, high-spirited type of country music.

Most requests of the raucous Perkins Brothers band were for hillbilly songs that the boys would jive up—classic Hank Williams standards infused with a faster rhythm. Carl ignited the songs with his black-oriented lead guitar playing; brother Clayton really chopped wood by slapping that bass fiddle; while brother Jay flogged his old acoustic guitar. As a result, the patrons drank even more cold beer and fired up the honky-tonk dance floor. This was honky-tonk employment security for the Perkins Brothers.

In July of 1954, when Carl first heard Elvis Presley's version of "Blue Moon of Kentucky," it amazed him to find the music so much like his own. Carl and his wife, Valda, heard Elvis on the radio and instantly knew that this rambunctious, barrier-shattering energy was right on par with the Perkins Brothers' own rocking style. Carl instantly recognized Elvis as a kindred spirit.

As Presley and his "Blue Moon of Kentucky" faded, the radio station disc jockey said, "That was Elvis Presley, a brand-new recording artist from Sam Phillips's Memphis-based Sun Records." Valda immediately turned to Carl and said, "There's a man down there in Memphis who understands what you're doing, and I think you need to go down there right now and see him."

A FRIEND NAMED FLUKE

W. S. Holland, a close friend of Carl's younger brother Clayton, had earned the nickname "Fluke" because his friends thought his life seemed full of unwitting surprises of amazing luck.

Fluke often visited the honky-tonks where the Perkin Brothers were playing. He sometimes stepped up on the platform stage next to his friend and kept rhythm by patting his hands in bongo-like drum patterns on the side of Clayton's bass fiddle. Carl loved the sound—and he also liked the old 1948 Cadillac limousine that W. S. owned. Carl repeatedly stated that he could just see "The Perkins Brothers Band" brightly painted on the side of that big old car.

One night Carl told Fluke to get a set of drums, because the Perkins Brothers band was going to Memphis to visit the recording studio where "that Elvis Presley fellow" got his start. Carl told W. S. he wanted him to come along and play drums. Years later W. S. laughed as he remembered the incident and said, "I don't know why he picked me. I asked Carl, 'What in the world would I do with a set of drums? I don't know how to play 'em.'"

"Well," Carl quickly answered, imagining how comfortable the trip to Memphis would be in that Cadillac, "Next week you *will* know how to play drums, and you'll play them on our recording session in Memphis." And then he added slyly, "By the way, I hope all our instruments will fit in your Cadillac."

Fluke smiled broadly as he finished the story: "So the next day—it was Sunday—I contacted a friend of mine who worked at a musical instrument store. We called him 'Slick' Glissen. Slick had some drums and could play pretty good, and he asked me the same thing. He said, 'Fluke, what you gonna do with them drums? You can't play 'em!' I firmly answered, 'Yeah, but I'll be playing them by Thursday.'"

So in early October 1954, Carl Perkins, his new drummer-in-training, W. S. "Fluke" Holland, and Carl's two brothers loaded up Holland's '48 Cadillac with all their musical instruments and headed for Sam Phillips's magic kingdom of Rockabilly at 706 Union Avenue, Memphis, Tennessee. They had tightly strapped the bass fiddle atop the old Caddy, carefully stacked the borrowed set of drums on top of Carl's guitar case in the trunk, and placed the amp right behind the front seat—as well as strategically positioned a jug of cheap whiskey between the two front seats, at-the-ready for taking the sting off the long drive. Anticipation soared as they thought of actually meeting the man who made Elvis Presley's recordings. So Carl Perkins and his sidekicks sped toward Rockabilly heaven—and, they hoped, a lofty place in music history.

A CHILLY RECEPTION

But no warm and friendly welcome awaited Carl Perkins and his band of players at Sun Records. Marion Keisker, Sam Phillips's faithful gatekeeper and Girl Friday, declared that Sun Records already had their boy, Elvis Presley, and they weren't interested in listening to anybody else. "Presley's hot!" she snapped.

Shaken by this outburst, Carl tried to explain that he and his brothers had a band that played the same kind of music as Elvis. His words fell on deaf ears. Marion continued to denounce Carl's proposal and emphatically said she could save him some time: "Sam Phillips, the owner, isn't here, and he wouldn't listen to you if he was here!"

Dazed, Carl quietly thanked Ms. Keisker and slowly shuffled his large frame out the door. Once on the sidewalk near the instrument-filled Cadillac, he spotted a brand-new, two-tone Cadillac Coupe de Ville as it anchored itself next to the curb. Carl immediately recognized that the driver's clothes exactly matched the colors of his car—dark blue pants with light blue on top. Carl muttered aloud for no one to hear, "This *has* to be Sam Phillips, 'cause no one but that Elvis Presley or Sam Phillips would be dressed just like his car."

Perhaps taking his cue from Israel's ancient King David, Carl reached for his imaginary slingshot and strategically positioned himself directly in Sam's path as the unamused Sun Records headmaster strolled toward the studio entrance. A very shy Carl Perkins gained inconceivable strength as he extended his hand and introduced himself to Phillips. Perkins, without waiting for the startled Sam Phillips to respond, continued his recitation by immediately segueing into the big question about auditioning for a record contract—a choreographed dance routine right out of Astaire's handbook.

Trying his best to maneuver around Carl's cotton patch frame, Sam caustically replied, "Man, I'm too busy. I'm not listening to anybody!" Then he tried another move around Carl to get to the sanctuary of his office.

"Mr. Phillips, please," Carl pleaded, as his hungry belly loudly rumbled. "Just listen to one or two of my songs, that's all. Man, you just don't know what that would mean to me."

Years later Sam Phillips recalled this historic encounter: "Carl seemed almost like he was gonna buckle to his knees in tears right there on the sidewalk. I was literally cornered by this crying hillbilly blocking the entrance of my studio—and well, I just couldn't turn him down."

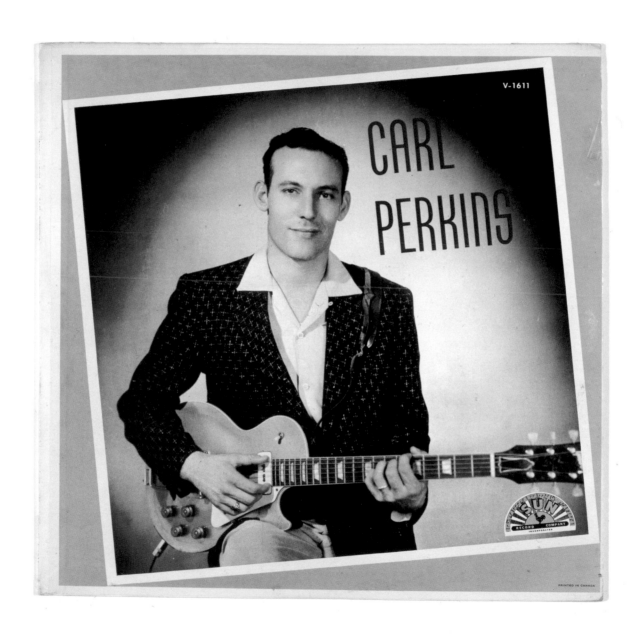

A LAST MOMENT SAVE

So the band got its chance. The boys set up right in the middle of the studio floor and nervously began to play. Brother Clayton was singing full throttle to the swift rhythm of one of Carl's original country songs when Sam yelled out, "That's too much like Ernest Tubb! We don't need another Ernest Tubb. You got anything else?" With each new song, Sam kept up his verbal barrage. Finally he could stand no more. Sam declared himself disgusted with this hillbilly bunch, dressed his vocabulary with strong language, told them explicitly where they should go, and proceeded to exit the building to quiet safety.

At that moment, Carl, trying to evade disaster, jumped to the microphone and began singing a melodic saga he had written for one of his girl-friends a few years before. It told the strange story of taking the girl to town for a picture show, riding on the back of a mule. The song had an original sound, and Carl thrust it along with his unique "Uncle John" guitar expertise.

Sam Phillips halted in midstride and re-entered the studio, standing inches away from the singer. Carl was really into the song by now and was moving around and gyrating in his desperation to please "this wild man who made Elvis."

Sam curtly stopped Carl and asked, "Can you sing that song standing still?" When Carl tried to explain himself, Phillips interrupted again with a gruff, "I want you to stand still in front of that microphone and sing this song again. I want to record it."

Shock overcame Carl and his players.

After a couple of tries, they finished the tune. As they packed up their instruments, Sam pulled Carl aside, looked him straight in the eyes, and said, "We're going to be great working together—but you don't want to let those other boys sing anymore. They really don't sing very good."

Years later, "Movie Magg"—the song about going to the movies on a mule—would become a favorite of The Beatles. The lyrics, however, confused them.

"We liked the sound," George Harrison told Carl, "but we never really understood what you were talking about when you sang about 'jumpin' on old Becky's back.' We couldn't figure out who Becky was."

"That was the name of the mule that me and my girl-friend rode to the picture show," Carl explained.

George Harrison, in particular, idolized Carl Perkins. In their early days together, The Beatles were notorious for giving each other nicknames. George wanted the other guys to call him Carl. "I was Carl Harrison," he said. "It's funny, really. Doesn't sound like a stage name right now; it's just that I loved Carl Perkins."

With "Movie Magg," Carl Perkins finally got his career moving. He never forgot that audition. Sam heard a soulfulness in Carl's voice that few others had. Sam also liked that Carl wrote most of the songs he performed. He believed Carl could rock, but to protect the position Elvis had carved out for Sam's struggling record company, Phillips insisted that Carl record *only* country music. Carl's first recording on Phillips's subsidiary label, Flip Records, was "Movie Magg," along with "Turn Around," released in February 1955.

THAT SONG HAS FED ME AND A BUNCH OF HUNGRY CHILDREN, SOME AUNTS AND UNCLES.
I'VE PAID OFF MORE '37 CHEVROLETS THAN ANY MAN IN TENNESSEE.

– CARL PERKINS

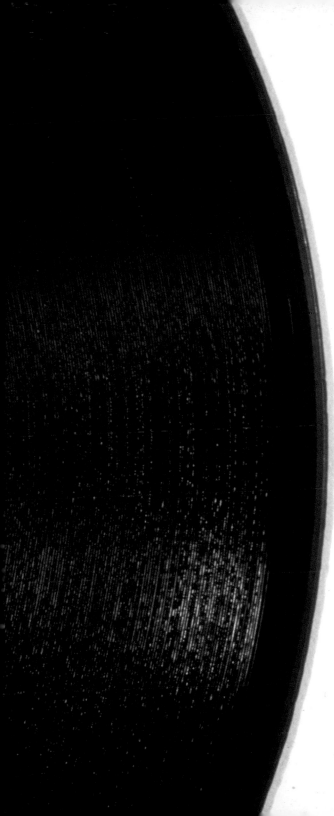

A SONG ABOUT SHOES

With the wax on Carl's "Movie Magg" still luke-warm, Johnny Cash joined the roster at Sun Records. Through most of 1955, Johnny and Carl toured with Elvis and other Louisiana Hayride acts throughout Texas and the South. Even though Carl's country records weren't selling well, Sam heard something special in them—especially Carl's "Let the Jukebox Keep on Playing" and "Gone, Gone, Gone." The latter was closest to the Rocka-billy style Carl craved and that had successfully launched Elvis's career the year before.

One night after a show in the fall of 1955, Johnny Cash told Carl about a black airman with whom he'd served in the air force. The airman really knew how to dress for weekend leave from their West German air base. Restricted from wearing civilian clothes, Johnny's friend often referred to his military regulation shoes as "blue suede shoes." Cash urged Carl to write a song about those shoes.

"I don't know anything about shoes," Carl objected. "How can you write a song about shoes?"

A few weeks later, Carl and the band were playing a small club near their home in Jackson, Tennes-see. Some students came into the club after their high school prom to dance. One young couple was dancing energetically near the front of the stage, right at the microphone where Carl was singing. Without warning, the boy jerked his pretty girl-friend by the arm and yelled, "Watch the suedes! Don't step on my suedes!" The young man's rude-ness really disturbed Carl, but the incident sud-denly reminded him of Johnny Cash's air force friend and the imaginary "blue suede shoes."

"I could not get that out of my mind," Carl remembered.

Carl returned home to his little government housing project and went to bed. About 2 a.m. he jumped out of bed and flew down the concrete steps, guitar in hand. "I thought of the old nurs-ery rhyme, 'One for the money, two for the show, three to get ready, and four to go.' And I said, 'Whoa,'" Carl remembered. Instantly in his hands the words became, "It's one for the money, two for the show, three to get to ready, now go man go."

Carl would later say it was the easiest song he ever wrote. He didn't have any writing paper, but quickly found an old pencil and dumped a few Irish potatoes out of a brown paper bag, flattened out the sack, and used it to write "Blue Swade, S-W-A-D-E."

"I couldn't even spell it right," he said.

Soon Carl's wife, Valda, appeared at the top of the steps. "Carl," she called out, "you're gonna wake up these babies—but whose song is *that*?"

"Well," he answered, "it's ours."

"You're writing that song?"

"Yeah."

"Well, you write the song. I'll rock the babies back to sleep."

Y
SHOW
get ready

TO CA

The precious and historic old brown paper sack on which Carl Perkins wrote the lyrics for his "Blue Swade Shoes" now resides on protected public display at the prestigious Smithsonian Institution in Washington D. C.

Excited about his new composition, Carl telephoned Sam Phillips the next day and sang a chorus of "Blue Suede Shoes" on the phone. At first, Sam reacted with his typically caustic attitude; but the more he heard, the more enthused he became.

Good thing, too. Although Sam appeared to be changing the world with his music, in fact he was getting in serious financial trouble. His record pressing bills were mounting, loans to his brother and friends were long overdue, and Sam needed money.

Elvis had signed a personal management contract with Bob Neal and Colonel Tom Parker, a slick promoter in partnership with country music legend Hank Snow. Parker had quite a reputation. He seemed very excited about Elvis and wanted to take complete control of the young phenom's personal management. Sam was quietly entertaining offers from major labels for his only major asset, Elvis. Parker put together a group to make Sam an offer he couldn't refuse. The Colonel got RCA Records and the publishing giant Hill and Range to jointly purchase Presley's contract from Phillips.

Parker struck a clever deal. Hill and Range was to front fifteen thousand dollars in exchange for the publishing rights on at least one side of every Presley record, as well as a copublishing deal on the Hi-Lo Music catalog owned by Sam Phillips. In all, Phillips received thirty-five thousand dollars from Parker, RCA, and Hill and Range; and in return, Sam had to pay Elvis five thousand dollars in back royalties. The final document also showed Parker as the sole manager of Presley—much to the disappointment of the Colonel's former partners, Bob Neal and Hank Snow, who vanished from the deal without receiving further compensation.

With Elvis off the Sun label and a little money in his pocket, Sam immediately called Carl to the studio on December 19, 1955, and uttered the words Carl longed to hear: "Carl Perkins, you're my Rockabilly cat now. Sing me that 'Blue Suede Shoes' song again."

Carl and his band got right to work in the studio. The first take was good, but a bit stiff. On the second take, however, Carl moved into another world. He sang the lyric like he was married to it, his guitar glowed with soulful perfection, and at the end of take two, Carl raised his head heavenward and said, "Thank you Uncle John Westbrook." To which Sam Phillips shouted enthusiastically, "We've got it!"

Plunging back to reality, Carl nervously told Sam that he wanted to do another take. He felt his lead guitar licks weren't up to par, and he suddenly recalled that he had sung the wrong lyric—"Go CAT go," rather than "Go MAN go." Sam sternly replied, "You ain't changing nothing. You burnt it! We're not changing anything. Smash, smash, smash—this record's a smash!"

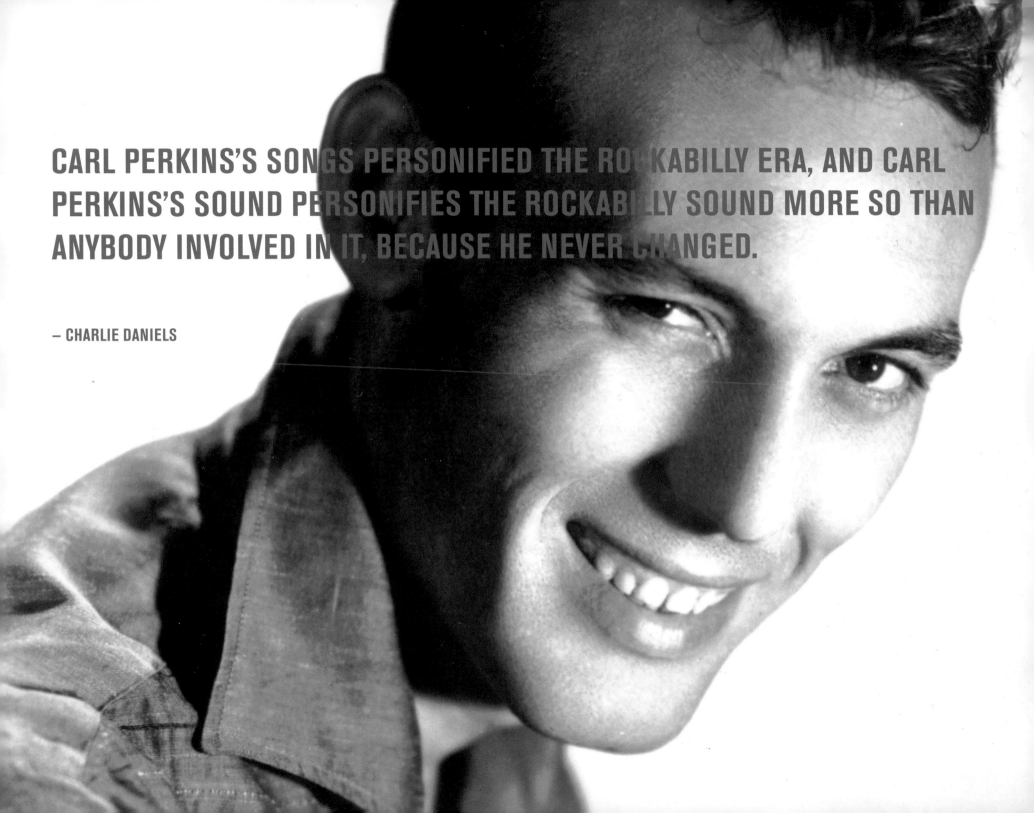

CARL PERKINS'S SONGS PERSONIFIED THE ROCKABILLY ERA, AND CARL PERKINS'S SOUND PERSONIFIES THE ROCKABILLY SOUND MORE SO THAN ANYBODY INVOLVED IN IT, BECAUSE HE NEVER CHANGED.

– CHARLIE DANIELS

Carl had never heard Phillips so excited, so completely carried away by a recording. The more Sam talked about "Blue Suede Shoes," the more his eyes glazed over—and then he began preaching like a Southern Baptist evangelist. Singing and shouting at the same time, Sam continued, "Carl Perkins has got a smash. Do you hear me, Perkins?" Sam was waving his arms high above his head, hands outstretched with his hair falling uncharacteristically out of place and onto his forehead. "Do you hear me, CARL PERKINS?!"

Carl's glazed eyes could see Phillips's antics, but he could no longer hear Sam rage. He had slipped back into that other place inside himself—back to the "before" with his mentor, Uncle John Westbrook. At that moment, what felt most significant to Carl was the wisdom of "Uncle John" that had guided his young life: "Let it *vi-ber-ate!* Keep prayin', Carl, God will hear you." The distant dreams, the hand-to-mouth life of the honky-tonk player, the pursuit of an elusive grail—all of it poured out onto the fret board of the Gibson Les Paul guitar as Carl's fingers found each note to tell his story and make his statement in the most personal and most dramatic of terms.

"I went off into deep water on the neck of that guitar on the second solo," Carl mused. "It's cookin'. I got somethin' outta this box I'd never got before."

Carl Perkins's "Blue Suede Shoes" was the first Rockabilly hit record to simultaneously reach number one on the country chart, number four on the pop chart, and number three in the rhythm and blues chart—a feat unprecedented in the record business.

Sam had once promised, "The first cat at Sun who sells me a million records, I'm gonna give him a new Fleetwood Cadillac." Sales for "Blue Suede Shoes" quickly exceeded a million, and true to his word, Sam handed over to Carl the keys and title to a new car. There was only one catch: Sam later deducted the cost of the "gift" Cadillac from Carl's personal record royalty account.

"You know, you hardly ever hear a Rockabilly song with just a little simple catgut string guitar," Carl later said. "You hear them with the band slap bass, the guitar and drums; but it wasn't written with those, come to think of it. It was me and a little cheap guitar that wrote the song, and it happened one night after I'd heard a boy tell a girl, 'Don't step on my suedes.' I said, 'Surely not. Surely he is not serious about that stupid shoe.' But he was, because he hurt her feelings. And from an old nursery rhyme that I played as a kid called Hide and Go Seek—I borrowed it. Thank you, Uncle John Westbrook."

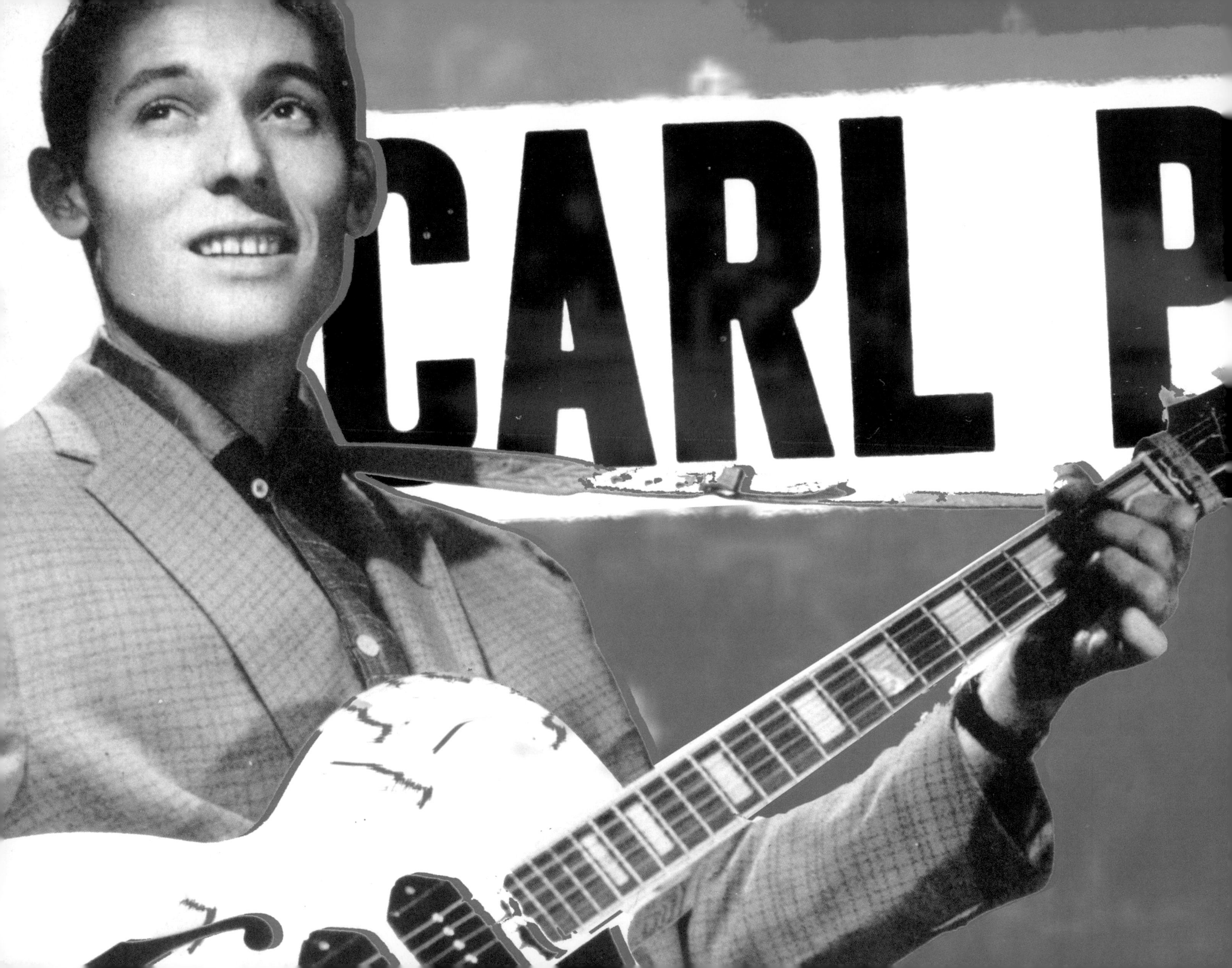
CARL P

ERKINS

NOBODY COULD SING HIS MUSIC LIKE HIM. A LOT OF FOLKS TRIED TO COVER HIS MUSIC, BUT CARL PERKINS WAS CARL PERKINS MUSIC, AND ANYTHING ELSE WAS AN IMITATION.

— GEORGE HUNT, CONTEMPORARY ARTIST

TRAGEDY ON THE ROAD

Sadly, Carl Perkins's rise to early stardom was about to dim in a most traumatic way. Carl, Clayton, Jay, and Fluke were scheduled to appear live on Perry Como's national network television show in New York City. During the all-night drive and just a few miles outside of Dover, Delaware, Carl's driver, Dick Stuart, fell asleep at the wheel and the car plowed head-on into a pickup truck.

When W. S. Holland woke up after the crash, he found Carl lying facedown in the muddy, water-filled ditch. Fluke grabbed a car seat from the wreckage and rolled Carl up on it. Carl woke up three days later in a hospital in Wilmington, Delaware—just eighty-five miles from New York City. Carl had suffered a fractured skull, fractured neck vertebra, and a broken arm. As he lay in bed, Perkins could hear men's voices, but couldn't turn his head to see where they came from. As he stared at the ceiling, he heard someone say, "I think he's the one that wrote it. I think he's the one that wrote that 'Blue Suede Shoes.' Two or three of 'em got killed."

In fact, only the driver of the truck, Thomas Phillips, had died. Jay Perkins suffered a broken neck and several internal injuries when he, like Carl, was thrown from the vehicle.

At the time of the accident, Carl's "Blue Suede Shoes" was jockeying with Elvis Presley's first RCA Records hit, "Heartbreak Hotel," for top position on the national charts. Presley reached number one three weeks after Carl's chart topper.

Although Elvis had promised Perkins that he wouldn't cover "Blue Suede Shoes" on a single record, just one month later RCA released Presley's first extended play 45 RPM record, which indeed included Carl's classic hit, coupled with "Tutti Frutti," "I've Got a Woman," and "Just Because." Although Carl's original Sun Records hit version of "Blue Suede Shoes" outsold Presley's RCA extended play cover, the song quickly became married to Presley.

"I watched Elvis perform on national network television as I was tethered to my bed in that Delaware hospital," Carl recalled. "They had me in a cast from my chin down to my waist. Elvis *shimmied* in front of that television camera and said, 'I'm gonna do a song from my new RCA record,' and then he sang, 'One for the money, a two for the. . . .'—and I nearly broke out of that cast. The room fell silent and my eyes went dark. And I said to myself, 'Ohhhh! There it goes!'"

Carl's record was still riding high on the charts when Elvis appeared on Milton Berle's *Stage Show* television program. Even when Carl had recovered enough to get back on the road, his record was still a mega-hit. "Blue Suede Shoes" remained on the national *Billboard* charts for five months and still casts an immense shadow on all of rock and roll. Who knows what might have happened had Carl been the first to sing this new brand of music on national television?

AN ENGLISH ADVENTURE

Carl toured England for the first time in 1964, coheadlining the tour with Chuck Berry and the two artists backed by the great band Eric Burden and The Animals. After the last night's performance of the tour, Carl and Chuck received an invitation to a party. Chuck bailed out of the invite right away, and Carl didn't want to go, explaining, "Man, I gotta go to Tennessee in the morning." But the promoter of the tour urged Carl in his best British manner, "You will most certainly want to go to this one."

So Carl went. As soon as he walked into the hall of this massive, beautiful mansion, someone tapped on an expensive crystal glass and everybody hushed. Then a man's voice said, "Ladies and gentlemen, he's here: Mr. Carl Perkins."

The party was for him.

Carl wound up sitting on the floor, sharing stories, playing guitar, and singing songs while surrounded by John, Paul, George, and Ringo of The Beatles. "Tomorrow night," they told him, "we're gonna be recording in the studios at Abbey Road, and we'd like you to come over."

Several things immediately ran through Carl's "old Rockabilly mind." *Man,* he thought, *here you are, in London, England, on a successful tour. You've just met what looks like the hottest group in world, with the number one song in America. You're a lucky man, Carl.*

And then Ringo said, "Mr. Perkins, would you care if I record some of your songs?"

Carl replied, "You want me to write you some songs?"

And Ringo answered, "I want to record 'Honey Don't.'"

"Man," Carl answered, "go ahead, have at it."

The totally out of the blue experience had a huge impact on Carl. "I shook," he said. "My soul shook. I left England with a completely different attitude. These guys gave me some strength that I needed at that time."

I WAS VERY LUCKY TO HAVE TWENTY-TWO YEARS
TO LOOK AT THE BACK OF MY OL' DADDY'S
HEAD, PLAYIN' WHILE I PLAYED THEM DRUMS.
I COULD TELL BY THE WAY HE TWISTED HIS
NECK WHAT HE WANTED TO DO NEXT. AND THE
BIGGEST PART OF THE TIME, I COULD HIT IT—
BE RIGHT THERE WITH HIM. HE SAW HIS NAME
IN LIGHTS, BUT YET HE WAS ABLE TO KEEP
THE SIMPLER THINGS IN LIFE AND LEAVE THIS
WORLD IN A FULFILLED WAY.

– CARL STANLEY PERKINS, SON OF CARL

THE WHOLE PACKAGE

Carl Perkins the entertainer was quite literally the whole package. He was the most dynamic guitar stylist for Rockabilly and fifties rock and roll, the consummate songwriter, and a great vocal stylist. People should listen more carefully to his recordings. He did things *differently*. He phrased songs differently. He had a different rhythm. He had a wonderful black-oriented sound, mixed in with some bluegrass and country.

"We took country songs and just put in the black rhythm, that black Southern gospel," Carl once said.

"He stayed focused," said Carl's son, Stan, about his dad's choice of musical style. "He put blinders on, just like them old mules that they used to use down in the fields. He put on those blinders and he stayed focused. This was what he wanted to do, and this would get him out of the cotton fields."

When you think of Carl Perkins, you have to think of the breadth and depth of his musical contributions. You think of the classic Rockabilly songs he wrote, now covered by hundreds of performers. You think of the songs he crafted for others, like "Daddy Sang Bass" for Johnny Cash, "Silver and Gold" for Dolly Parton, or the song he wrote with Paul McCartney, "Get It."

Carl Perkins the guitar player overshadowed all of his contemporaries at Sun Records and influenced rock star guitarists like Eric Clapton and George Harrison, among others. He truly is the godfather of Rockabilly music.

Carl Lee Perkins: April 9, 1932 - January 19, 1998

THE ONLY MUSIC WE WANTED TO MAKE

IT WAS ROY ORBISON WHO DESCRIBED THE PLEASURE HE FELT IN THE FREEDOM TO CREATE THE ONLY KIND OF MUSIC HE WANTED TO MAKE, BUT I'M SURE LOTS OF OTHER ROCKABILLY STARS COULD HAVE ECHOED HIS COMMENTS. TWO LEGENDS IN PARTICULAR COME TO MIND: JOHNNY CASH AND JERRY LEE LEWIS. WITHOUT QUESTION, BOTH COULD HAVE SAID EXACTLY THE SAME THING.

"Johnny Cash has always been the kind of guy that is liked by everybody," declared Cash's friend Charlie Daniels. "I mean, certain artists are liked by this segment of the population, this age demographic, these teenagers, younger people, so on and so forth—doctors, lawyers, professional people. I mean, Johnny Cash is LOVED by college students and people in geriatric homes. And if there has ever been a great artist, *Johnny Cash is a great, great artist!*"

In 1986, Johnny Cash leaned into the microphone and with his best signature voice said, "Hello, I'm Johnny Cash." I felt frozen in silence, awaiting the massive roar in response from his loyal fans—a response I'd heard countless times, but a mere trick in my head this time around, since we were alone in the studio.

John brought me back to reality as he continued his story: "The very first song I learned to sing was 'I Am Bound for the Promised Land.' This grand old gospel favorite was forever embedded in my young mind by my mother. She sang it over and over with us kids during that late night ride in the old flatbed truck when we moved the family over to Dyess, Arkansas. It was in 1934. I was only two years old, but somehow I remembered. I believe the struggle of that family move from our Great Depression-era failed cotton farm to the federal government subsidized cooperative cotton fields, made a deep impression on me, even at that age, 'cause I never forgot the late night trip nor mother's old gospel anthem."

The Cash family attended the little First Baptist Church in the Dyess community, where Carrie Cash, Johnny's mother, played piano for the services. J. R., as Johnny was named at birth, at first felt frightened by the preacher's shouting and the congregation's emotional weeping during the worship services, but he loved the music. Carrie encouraged her young son to learn to sing all the old gospel songs and, through them, John began to better understand the preacher's sermons. With his mother's gentle prompting, a very young J. R. Cash kept singing. She heard something *special* in his voice. John began to use these songs as a way to pray—something that stayed with him all his life. And it didn't hurt a bit to have a little radio around the house.

"Late at night," John continued, "while my older brother, Jack, was studying his Bible, I used to listen to the country music stations and gospel stations on the radio. As I listened, I dreamed. That was what I wanted to be—a singer on that radio."

Johnny dearly loved Jack, who was studying to become a preacher. Jack nurtured his younger brother's spiritual life and led Johnny to become a Christian at a young age. For the rest of his life, Johnny mourned Jack's untimely death—he was killed in a power saw accident while the two were still boys. Had Jack lived to witness the reality of Johnny's dream, however, he might well have marked this special occasion with a quote from God's Word. I think of him honoring his brother with a sentence from Acts, chapter 13 and verse 22: "...a man after my own heart; he will do everything I want him to do." Brother Jack knew the reality of his younger brother's faith, and even at that early age, Jack thoroughly believed that Johnny would always "Walk the Line."

Five decades later, John Carter Cash, the son of Johnny and June Carter Cash, put his own exclamation mark on his father's matchless life by declaring, "His greatest legacy has been his love of God. Without Dad's love of God, none of this would ever have happened."

BLACK

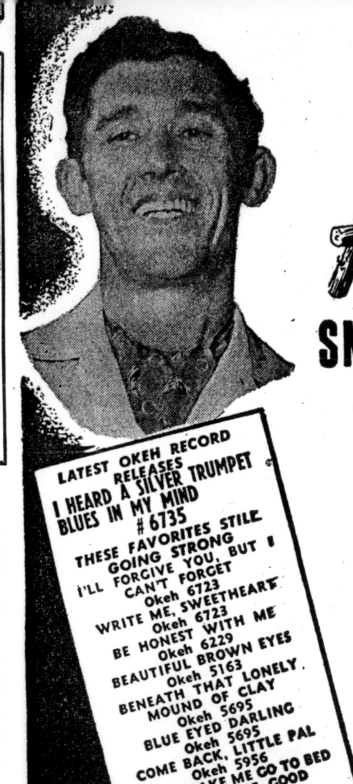

A VARIETY OF MUSICAL INFLUENCES

Johnny liked a wide variety of music: The honky-tonk hillbilly music of Hank Williams, Ernest Tubb, Roy Acuff, and Eddy Arnold; Southern gospel blues from Rosetta Tharpe; bluegrass gospel from Bill Monroe and Ira and Charlie (The Louvin Brothers). Cash also liked the swing sound of the big bands, with Bing Crosby and the Andrews Sisters.

What influenced Johnny Cash the most, however—just as it had Carl Perkins—was the haunting sound of the Grand Ole' Opry from Nashville, Tennessee. Every Saturday night, the live music wafting over that little battery powered radio brought the Carter Family and Jimmie Rodgers to a young Johnny, infusing within him the soulful foundation of the Appalachian and Southern folk styles of music.

"Nothing in the world was more important to me than hearing those songs on the radio," Johnny insisted. "This was the music and these were the great artists who helped me learn how to later tell real *song-stories* from personal experiences and places and things I'd felt and seen."

Johnny often said that The Louvin Brothers live show, which he got to see as a teenager at his Dyess High School auditorium, was the turning point of his life. "Nobody would believe me when I'd say, 'I'll be up there someday. That's what I'm gonna be.' I had no doubt about it. And Mother knew it, too! She had that same feeling—she'd say, 'J. R., you're gonna be a singer on that radio.'"

SAM CASHES IN ON CASH

While stationed in Germany during a four-year stint in the air force, Johnny formed a little hillbilly band that performed in the base's service clubs. This gave J. R. a good opportunity to learn how to improve his guitar playing and how to write songs.

"All I ever wanted to do was sing," Johnny passionately declared. "I tried a few places when I first got out of the air force, and I couldn't get a break. So I entered the radio announcing school in Memphis, Tennessee: Keegan School of Broadcasting. And I'd been going five months, half-time, when I finally got Sam Phillips to listen."

Motivated by Elvis Presley's success, Johnny phoned Sam Phillips at Sun Records and tried to make an appointment for an audition. He didn't get the reception he'd hoped for.

"I was put off and turned down," Johnny recalled. "So one day I just turned up on his steps with my guitar in hand—and believe it or not, Sam let me through that door to audition for him."

In his first audition with Phillips, Johnny pulled out his strongest gospel song at the time, "Belshazzar," a real up-tempo mover. Johnny put everything he had into it for Sam. After this unique guitar-vocal performance, Phillips lost some of his caustic negativism and wanted to hear more. "What else have you got?" he demanded. It was if Johnny had allowed Sam to peek ever-so-slightly into his soul—and Sam felt haunted by what he saw and heard. He, too, heard something special in Johnny's voice.

But when Johnny didn't immediately have what Sam was looking for, the maverick record producer looked the young singer straight in the eyes and said, "Go home and sin a little bit. Write me some songs like Elvis Presley is recording. Bring those songs back and we'll record them."

"GO HOME AND SIN A LITTLE BIT. WRITE ME SOME SONGS LIKE ELVIS PRESLEY IS RECORDING. BRING THOSE SONGS BACK AND WE'LL RECORD THEM."

Johnny didn't immediately take Sam up on his challenge, but he did return to Sun Records the next day for a second audition. He trotted out "Hey Porter," a song he wrote during his air force years from 1950 to 1954. That poem, inspired by the trains that ran behind his family's small share-cropper house in Arkansas, had been published in the armed forces magazine *Stars and Stripes*. It wasn't one of John's favorites, but he thought Sam might like it better than the others. Phillips didn't jump up and down when he heard it, but he decided this was the song to start with.

"Bring your boys in tomorrow," Sam ordered, "and we'll record that song."

The "boys" Sam referred to included Luther Perkins on electric guitar, Marshall Grant on slap bass, and A. W. "Red" Kernodle on steel guitar. They had been playing gospel and country music at local church pie socials and on local Memphis radio with some good response. They called their group "The Tennessee Three."

The next day, however, when Cash and his Tennessee Three set up for the recording session, started tuning their instruments, and struggled through the song, each band member got so nervous that his talent seemed to evaporate. Sam got annoyed, then agitated. Clearly, he was not amused. Red felt so overcome with Sam's outbursts, in fact, that he quickly packed up his steel guitar and retreated out of the studio before the group made it through the entire song even once. That left only Luther Perkins on lead guitar and Marshall on bass to support their friend Johnny Cash.

Cash's star rose quickly with Luther Perkins on the guitar. "Had there been no Luther Perkins," Charlie Daniels claims, "there may not have been a Johnny Cash. I mean, you could hear Luther start playing that guitar intro to one of their songs, and immediately you know it's going to be Johnny Cash."

Still, on that day so long ago, Sam felt more than a little nervous about the number of takes the recording required (mostly because of Luther's lead guitar mistakes); but on the other hand, Luther clearly had something magically different brewing. And Johnny's powerful vocal delivery emphasized his mystical and surly voice—you could almost see the words flying out of his mouth and pummeling the microphone. Pure magic lived in this Johnny Cash debut recording . . . and then Sam added his signature slap-back echo, marinating J. R.'s vocal perfection in the tasty sauce of Rockabilly.

But like so many other stories about Rockabilly's roots, this would be providential—the beginning of that unique, sparse sound that made Johnny Cash a recognizable icon around the world. Since they had no drums, Sam came up with the idea of weaving a strip of paper between the strings of Johnny's acoustic rhythm guitar and having him play his chords higher up on the neck. This gave the trio an eerie, almost brushstroke-like snare drum sound, which helped to fill out the overall instrumentation. This "paper trick" guitar rhythm sound—which everyone in early Rockabilly later tried to replicate—became one of Johnny Cash's "secret weapons."

With Sam Phillips's engineering genius, Cash and The Tennessee Two soon developed a unique sound that followed them for thirty years. Cash's ragged, rugged baritone was mixed up front of the instruments, with the tape delay slap-back echo laid heavy over both the voice and Luther Perkins's *boom-chicka* guitar licks. Behind them, Marshall flailed away at the slap bass, generating lumbering rhythm support like a locomotive hurtling down the rails. He really worked that bass, slappin' the neck and poppin' the strings with everything he had.

IN SEARCH OF MEMORIES

On the early morning of October 4, 2005, I wandered into the woods near Old Hickory Lake in Hendersonville, Tennessee, with our small production crew. This morning would present one of our biggest challenges.

John Carter Cash was up with the daylight, and the smell of his fresh-brewed coffee met us before we arrived at the door. The Johnny Cash Log Cabin Studio sat silent in the early morning light, just steps from the home of Johnny and June Carter Cash. Though both legends are now gone, I could still feel the presence of family in that cabin. An eerie hush settled on our group as we approached. When my feet actually touched the flat boards of the place, my heart raced with anticipation.

From 1979 until his death, Johnny Cash frequently came to this Old Hickory Lake cabin to write, to meditate, to play his guitar, to sing, to shout, to pray, or to just sit silently and remember. I prayed, too—for a sharper memory. I wanted to recall how it really was at the beginning. I longed to piece together the close relationships between Cash and Johnny Horton, Elvis, Carl Perkins, Bob Luman, Tillman Franks, and so many more of us who broke the ice together back in the fifties on those classic Hayride tours. I could almost feel his presence—in fact, everyone did. Johnny Cash was always bigger than life, and now with his passing, he seems bigger than death.

I broke the silence and asked John Carter Cash to "explain" his father. John breathed out a long sigh and quietly said, "Well, my father is a man of variations, paradoxes, and extremes. There is no doubt, even though he was a shy person, inside he had an energy that could not be bridled. He would take to the stage and suddenly become Johnny Cash. My father had a way of appealing to the world with that energy—you know, a way of reaching into the heart of people."

It was true. Everybody loved Johnny Cash, and not just because he was a great performer. At that point, my early days of knowing and loving Johnny Cash just sort of fell out of my brain and onto my lips, and I found myself saying the obvious to John Carter Cash: "I knew your dad pretty well, starting at fifteen years of age when I first met him and worked with him on The Louisiana Hayride. You also know that we had some times, when we were older, that we lived life on the edge a little bit. But your dad did everything—everything, under the circumstances—with dignity."

I asked John Carter Cash to revisit with me the music of the fifties. The early Johnny Cash music is nothing short of incredible. I think of the Sun Masters: "Cry, Cry, Cry," "Hey Porter," "I Walk the Line," "Folsom Prison," "Ballad of a Teenage Queen." The list goes on and on. I asked the son of my old friend to give me his thoughts about how all that magic came out of his father.

John slowly looked around the cabin, as if he were surveying the legacy his dad left, sighed a huge sigh, and cautiously measured his words. "Well, you know," he began, "to say where the Johnny Cash magic of creativity comes from, or to define it, is probably close to impossible. It's hard to say where it came from. One could say it comes from pain—like it came from him losing his brother in that saw blade accident at such a young age. One can say that it came from the hardships of workin' in those cotton fields of Arkansas, from the dark days of his depression in his youth, from his hunger for a more loving relationship with his dad, or from the separation from his family when he was overseas in Germany in the air force. We can try to define it, but to do so may lessen the mystique of my dad."

He then smiled slightly and declared, "You wanna look for answers, but maybe the mystery of Johnny Cash is just as strong—just as important. My dad had a great creative spark in him and persistence in his character that continued until the day he passed. He didn't know how to stop. In the face of pain, in the face of struggle, loss, whatever, he didn't quit. And that was as evident in the very beginning of his career creatively—in his love life, in his music life, in his performance life—as it was at the end of his life."

I think my late friend's modesty might have caused him to shuffle a bit to hear such comments from his son, but my personal knowledge of Johnny Cash—as a man and as a father—tells me that he would feel proud of his boy, John Carter Cash. Johnny Cash never had any trouble revealing his deepest desires, either verbally or musically.

"YOU WANNA LOOK FOR ANSWERS, BUT MAYBE THE MYSTERY OF JOHNNY CASH IS JUST AS STRONG—JUST AS IMPORTANT. MY DAD HAD A GREAT CREATIVE SPARK IN HIM AND PERSISTENCE IN HIS CHARACTER THAT CONTINUED UNTIL THE DAY HE PASSED. HE DIDN'T KNOW HOW TO STOP. IN THE FACE OF PAIN, IN THE FACE OF STRUGGLE, LOSS, WHATEVER, HE DIDN'T QUIT. AND THAT WAS AS EVIDENT IN THE VERY BEGINNING OF HIS CAREER CREATIVELY—IN HIS LOVE LIFE, IN HIS MUSIC LIFE, IN HIS PERFORMANCE LIFE—AS IT WAS AT THE END OF HIS LIFE."

- JOHN CARTER CASH

THE FIRST TIME I MET JOHNNY CASH WAS ON THIS STAGE HERE AT THE RYMAN AUDITORIUM.
HE WAS THE MOST EXCITING THING I HAD EVER SEEN. HE WAS LIKE LIGHTNING.
HE WAS LIKE A PANTHER PROWLING AROUND THIS PLACE—AND DANGEROUS LOOKING.

– KRIS KRISTOFFERSON, SINGER, SONGWRITER, ACTOR, AND FRIEND

A LOOK BEHIND THE HITS

We all know the songs, but how did they come to be? Johnny detailed his writing of "Cry, Cry, Cry" like this:

I didn't have "Cry, Cry, Cry" written at the first session. Sam asked me to go home and write an up-tempo love song. So, I got home that night and wrote "Cry, Cry, Cry."

There was a disc jockey named Smilin' Eddy Hill that I listened to on the radio every night. He was really a character and he'd say, "Okay folks, we're gonna cry, cry, cry all night long. Here's a weeper." So, that night as I was listening to old Smilin' Eddy Hill on the radio, I wrote "Cry, Cry, Cry" pretty quickly. I brought it in to Sam the next day and he really liked it.

Cash and the Tennessee Two rushed back to the studio the very next day with the new song Johnny had written. "Cry, Cry, Cry" fit the bill perfectly as the B-side for his first single record on Sun, "Hey Porter." Phillips released the record in June, 1955, and this initial outing for Johnny Cash and the Tennessee Two reached the number fourteen position of the *Billboard* national country music charts. It also forever imprinted the core *boom-chicka-boom-chicka*, steady-cadenced rhythm and sound of Johnny Cash's recordings.

Besides "Hey Porter," Johnny also had written "Folsom Prison Blues" while stationed at Landsberg Air Force Base in West Germany. He wrote the song after watching a movie about the tough life of a prisoner in Folsom Prison, one of the oldest and toughest penal institutions in California. Tired of the heavy drinking in his squadron and overcome with dark notions in his own heart, Cash decided to write the song from the perspective of an un-remorseful killer. Somehow he came up with what became the best-known and most descriptive line of the song: "I shot a man in Reno, just to watch him die." Cash says of the writing, "I sat with the pen in my hand and tried to think of the worst reason a person could have for killing another person, and that's what came to mind."

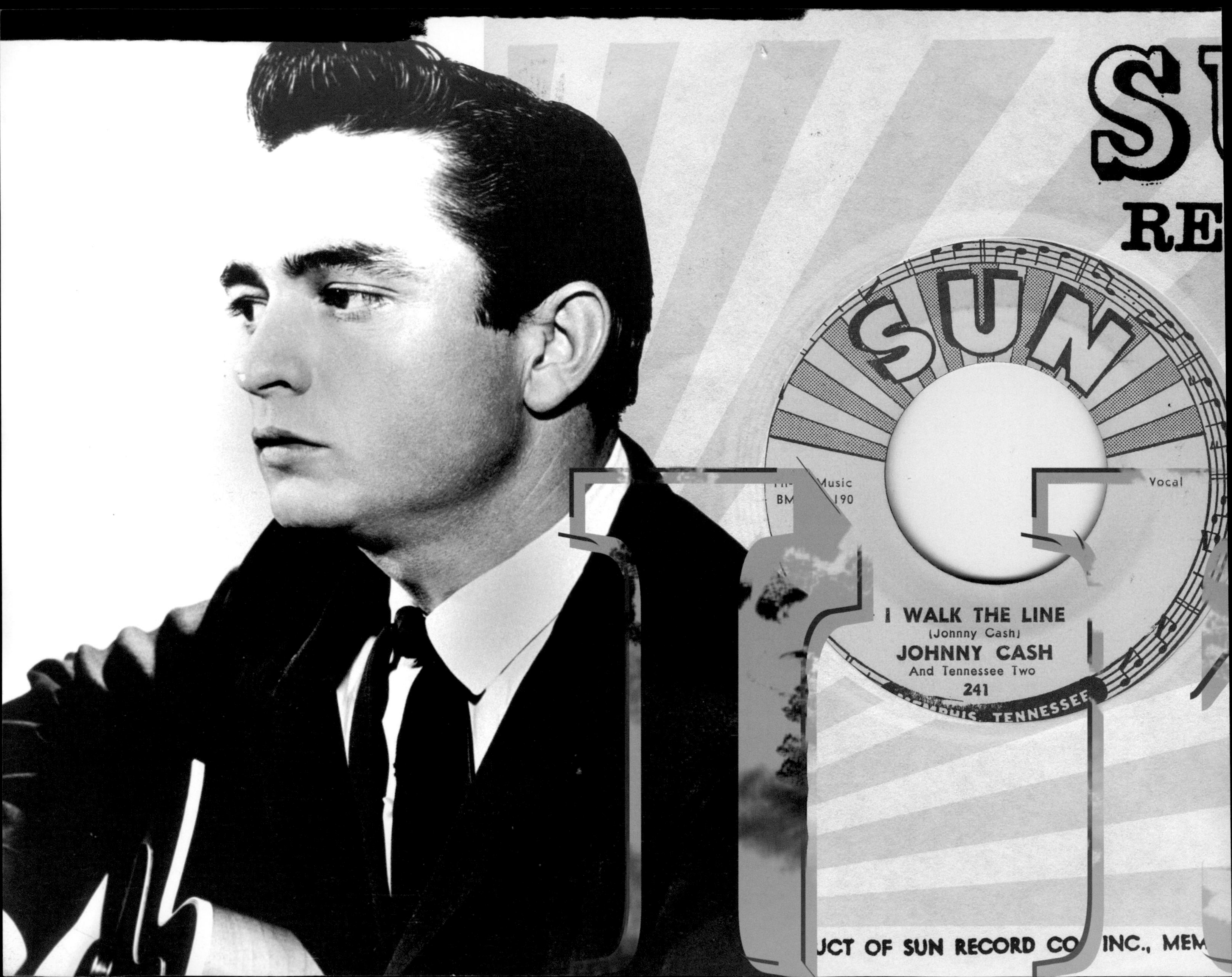

SUN
Vocal
I WALK THE LINE
(Johnny Cash)
JOHNNY CASH
And Tennessee Two
241
TENNESSEE
UCT OF SUN RECORD CO INC., MEM

"I Walk the Line," on the other hand, was Johnny's personal oath to himself to stay true to his family, his friends, and his strong Christian faith. He wrote the melody while in West Germany and had the title-hook of the song, "Because you're mine," rolling around in his head for months. One night he and his good friend Carl Perkins were exchanging creative ideas about songs, and Johnny sang the lyric: "I keep a close watch on this heart of mine, because you're mine, I walk the line." Carl quickly declared, "I think 'I Walk the Line' would be a better title." What a great payback to Johnny Cash for earlier firing up Carl to write a song about some "Blue Suede Shoes"!

"I Walk the Line," released in 1956, became Cash's first major hit. Sam Phillips had sold Elvis Presley's contract to RCA Records for thirty-five thousand dollars and used the funds to promote both "Blue Suede Shoes" and "I Walk the Line." Johnny's song rocketed to number one on the national country music charts, reached number seventeen on the pop charts, and by the end of the year had sold more than two million copies.

At this point you should remember that Sam Phillips had stated publicly that he would give a brand-new Cadillac Fleetwood to whatever Sun artist would sell a million records. While he made good on his promise (sort of) to Carl Perkins, he never did give Johnny his new car when "I Walk the Line" more than doubled the target number. That broken promise caused some real friction between the two men and eventually became one reason why both Johnny Cash and Carl Perkins left Sun Records for new recording contracts with Columbia Records.

I THINK IT WAS JOHNNY'S INTEGRITY AND HIS CREATIVE FIRE THAT MADE HIM SO SUCCESSFUL, BUT ABOVE ALL IT WAS LIKE HE REPRESENTED THE TRUTH AND I WOULD HAVE BELIEVED EVERYTHING HE SAID—WELL, NOT EVERYTHING HE SAID. JOHN HAD A PRETTY CREATIVE IMAGINATION, TOO. BUT WHEN IT WAS SOMETHING THAT MATTERED, JOHNNY CASH WAS THE TOUCHSTONE THAT IS THE TRUTH.

— KRIS KRISTOFFERSON, SINGER, SONGWRITER, ACTOR, AND FRIEND

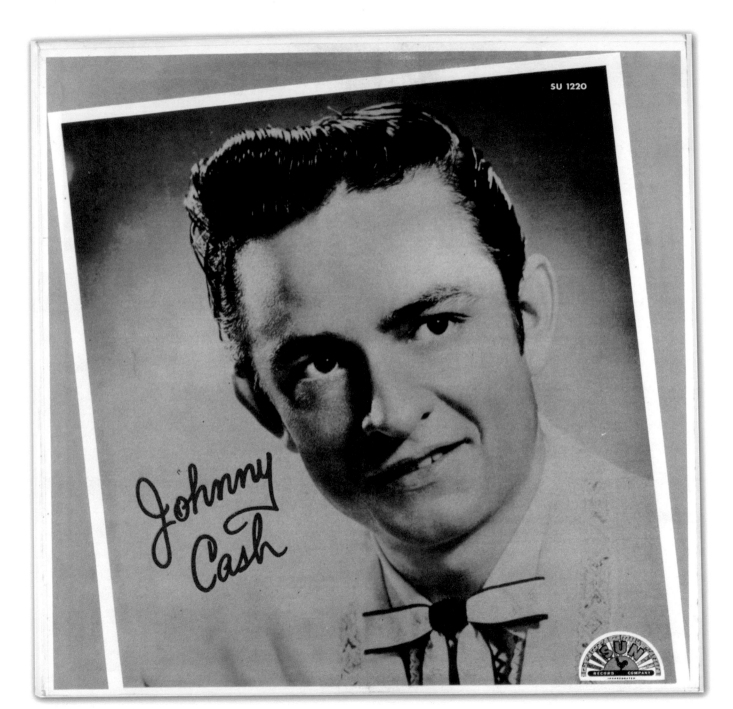

I STOOD AND WATCHED JOHNNY CASH BECOME THE SUPERSTAR.
I WATCHED A MAN STANDING FLAT-FOOTED AND BECOME A GIANT.
I LOVE HIM TO THIS DAY AND I ALWAYS WILL.

– CARL PERKINS

DARK DAYS FOR A GOOD GUY

Johnny Cash placed at least two hit singles a year on the *Billboard* national music charts for thirty-three straight years, and more than fifty-three million copies of his albums have sold since 1959. The man knew how to make an impression!

Sam Phillips used to sit around and regale visitors with how great a person Johnny Cash was. Johnny quickly became Sam's fair-haired boy. Sam really admired Johnny, and he loved to talk about the authority of his young singer's voice; it just drew people to him.

Yet Johnny himself admitted that in the amazing flurry of his success, he gradually lost his way. By the sixties he had begun to tour more than three hundred days a year, had divorced, and had become dependent on amphetamines. In 1968 he married June Carter, and with her help and encouragement, he made a remarkable recovery. A pair of live recordings at Folsom Prison and San Quentin both went gold.

"Drugs are so deceptive," he once said. "It's like a demon that says, 'Hey, I'm so pretty, look at me, I'll make you feel better! Take me.' And I do. It's a battle. I've talked to those pills. There'd be six of 'em and I'd say, 'I'm just gonna take one of you today,' and I could almost hear them saying, 'No, you're gonna take all of us.' 'Cause when you're on that stuff, one is too many and a thousand is not enough."

Johnny Cash died on September 12, 2003.

HE TAUGHT US ALL

Johnny Cash was a special friend and a really good guy. God blessed him with a wonderful, innocent, raw talent. I think he taught all of us the importance of simplicity, the necessity of being gentle with a song or prudent in writing the lyrics of that song. Johnny Cash was a true troubadour. They say he was America's greatest folk singer, and I guess that's true. But he certainly was the lone *solitary man*.

"I think some of the old-timers in the business had a lot more vision about what this is all about than some of the people who were running the business," he once said. "I was encouraged to do it the way I felt it, by people like Ernest Tubb. He told me, 'You're different, you sound different, you act different, you look different; if that's the way you honestly feel it, then that's the way you want to do it, and don't let anybody change you.'"

Johnny Cash truly is an American icon. He blurred the boundaries of all genres of music and made it all Johnny Cash. From Corriganville to Carnegie Hall, he was and still is Johnny Cash.

In an interview for our *Rockabilly Legends* documentary, Johnny defined himself better than anyone else ever could by recalling the signing of his first Sun

"The day I signed my first recording contract with Sam Phillips," he recalled, "I only had fifteen cents to my name. When I left the Sun Studio, there was a panhandler sitting on the street begging for money. A loaf of bread and a package of cigarettes each cost twenty cents, and I didn't have enough money for either one. So, as I walked by the beggar, I gave him my last fifteen cents and I walked away a happy man."

Johnny Cash, honored as one of the pioneers of Rockabilly and fifties rock and roll, was inducted into the Rock and Roll Hall of Fame and Museum in 1992.

J.R. "Johnny" Cash: February 26, 1932 - September 12, 2003

SPONTANEOUS COMBUSTION

While Johnny Cash's success on "I Walk the Line" depended on his own enormous talent and that of the Tennessee Two, it probably didn't hurt that a piano-playing wild man from Ferriday, Louisiana—a newcomer to Sun Records—worked behind the scenes on that recording session.

That wild man, Jerry Lee Lewis, would soon become a household name worldwide, joining the Sun Records Rockabilly royalty of Elvis Presley, Carl Perkins, Johnny Cash, and Roy Orbison.

And what a notorious wild man he is, this Jerry Lee Lewis! He does things to a piano that would be against the law in a lot of states. He gets up on it and plays it with his hind-side and his elbows and his feet—I mean, he does it *all*. He sends the piano bench sailing side-over-bottom with a kung fu kick that would humble Jackie Chan. He lifts the lid of the grand, shakes his head, shakes his legs, shakes his hair, shakes his whole self. Then, with incendiary stealth, he sprays the piano with a bit of flammable liquid and, as sud-

Yes, it's a fact: he literally does *set the piano on fire*!

Suddenly, there's screaming! Yelling! Stomping of feet! Clapping of hands! Crying! Singing! And yet, no one gets worried (except maybe the owner of the piano). No one is scared (except maybe the fire department). No one runs away (except maybe the piano tuner). Just the opposite! Crazed fans rush the stage, trying to get as close as they can to this wild man, to their hero, to their Rockabilly idol.

He's *The Killer*!

Not since Wolfgang Amadeus Mozart has there been anyone remotely like the cheeky, the momentous, the erratic, the egocentric, the ostentatious, the amazingly creative genius of The Killer. Jerry Lee Lewis joins Amadeus in the outrageous fraternity of the irreverent.

"His unique, self-designed piano-playing style is a primal force of modern music—his versatility as renowned as his originality. Jerry Lee Lewis mixes genres in much the same way as he weaves complexity into his syncopated rhythmic patterns on the piano. By his own admission, God directs his left hand to play a *Cousin Carl McVoy*-inspired, rock-solid boogie-woogie, while Lewis' right hand plays the upper register keys with unmatchable flamboyant filigree and brazenness. He naturally blends equal parts gospel fervor and wild showmanship," wrote renowned music composer and syndicated writer Cub Koda.

NOTHING LIKE HIM

By all measures, even at a precocious fourteen years of age, Jerry Lee Lewis's piano genius was as good as it could ever get. Already he was primed for center stage.

The Killer *always* sounded good. He has a great beat and a unique feel on the piano. Everybody loves his animated music, and his hits are classic rock and roll, all solid gold and platinum. He's one-of-a-kind.

Jerry Lee Lewis's notorious exploits as the piano-bashing *wildman extraordinaire* allowed him to literally write the book on impertinence and arrogance. To read of anything remotely similar, you have to delve into reports of the centuries-old extravagance and infamy of his notorious classical counterpart, Wolfgang Amadeus Mozart. Surely these were two of the most significant music geniuses God ever created.

Contemporary artist George Hunt weighs in on Jerry Lee: "Jerry Lee Lewis sits well on my canvas. The Killer is still the KILLER!! Short fused—quick to anger. He wants everything just right, and when it goes right, you get a show that you will remember for an eternity!"

Hunt ponders this musical meteor and declares, "You know, where most people touch a piano very gingerly, Jerry Lee just beats the stuffin' out of it—the first guy I've ever seen doin' that. I don't see how they kept the ivory on the keys the way he plays. Jerry Lee Lewis strikes me, from an artist's perspective, as being an arrogant person. What's wrong with that? He's an artist. He knows what he wants and he can't take second best. Some other people may think he's arrogant or kind of crazy, but that's just the genius in the individual that's on display. That's just Jerry Lee Lewis being Jerry Lee Lewis."

I agree wholeheartedly with my good friend George Hunt. There's Jerry Lee Lewis, and then there's everybody else!

IN THE BEGINNING...

God delivered Jerry Lee Lewis to the world on September 19, 1935, into the faithful arms of Mamie and Elmo Lewis, devout Christians and devoted members of the local Assembly of God congregation. Jerry Lee grew up on a small farm near the community of Ferriday, Louisiana, and could not escape either his Southern upbringing or his strong Pentecostal church foundation.

Jerry Lee tells his own story the best: "I have two sisters, Linda Gail and Frankie Jean, and I have cousins and more cousins. I also have aunts and uncles. That's where all those cousins come from. It's a big family. And, we're a *very close* family—closer than most, but much like all close families around the South; cousins, double-cousins, and even triple-cousins. We all went to church together on Sunday—morning and night—and prayer meetings on Wednesday nights. The preacher preached right to you. The piano player played and the singers sang. I loved all that. I was raised in a Christian home and I am a Christian-minded person. That's just the way I am."

Lewis, never lost for words, continued to recount his own legend:

My Mother and Daddy took out a loan on the farm and bought me a well-used secondhand piano when I was eight—and I started right in playing it. I'd go to school, and then I'd come home and play the piano. I taught myself. It was a gift from God. Other people practice and they practice. These fingers of mine, they got brains in 'em. You don't tell them what to do. They just do it—God-given talent. I never heard anybody play piano that I thought I wanted to copy after.

My cousins—more like my brothers, Jimmy Swaggart and Mickey Gilley—played that old Stark piano all the time with me and we took lessons together. We'd go down to the black church and peek in the window or crawl under the church and listen to the piano playing. We could feel it real good. We learned a lot from that.

We also sneaked into Haney's Big House juke joint across the tracks, which only catered to the black people. Haney's was owned by our uncle Lee Calhoun. Uncle Lee'd let us sneak in and hide in a dark corner under a table so we could feel the music. It was like getting vaccinated with that rhythm. We all three played piano in church, one at a time, of course. But we played those old gospel songs with some rhythm. Everybody in the choir was trying to keep up with us. We played that spiritual style like they did down at the little black church and at Haney's. The preacher scolded, "Boys, you're pushin' it a bit too much! Better slow it back down." They'd never heard nothin' like that down there.

So the Jerry Lee Lewis story starts and ends with The Killer "pushing the envelope" to the razor's edge . . . and always a bit more.

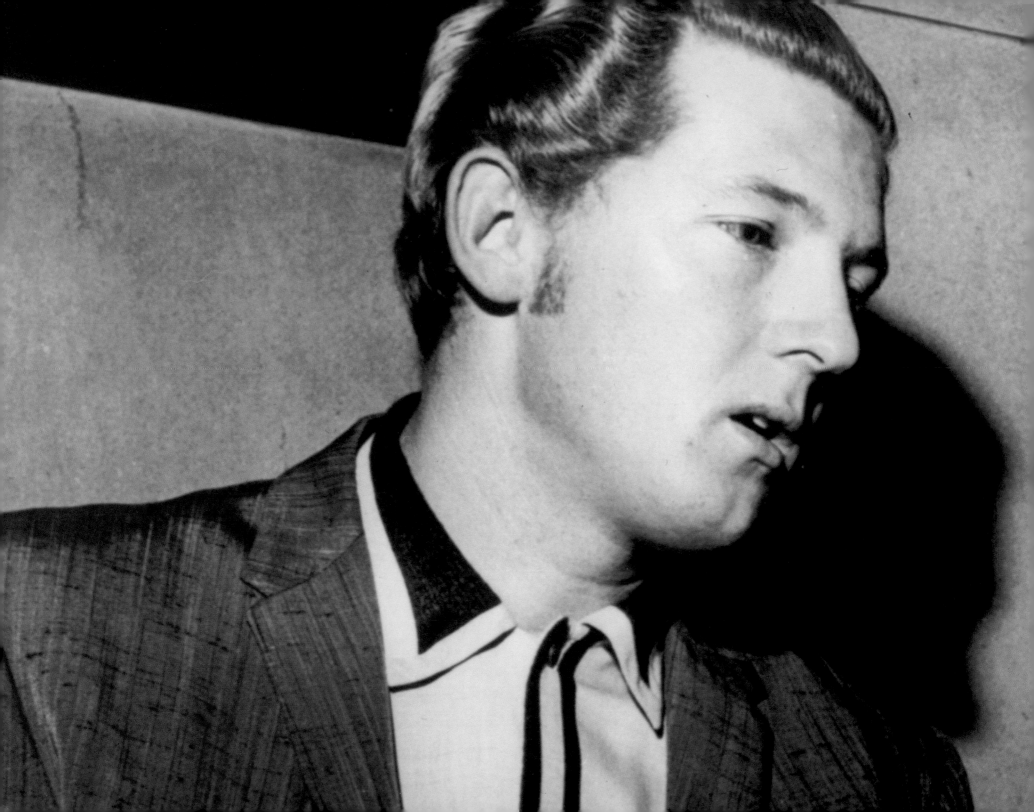

Jerry Lee and his sister Linda Gail

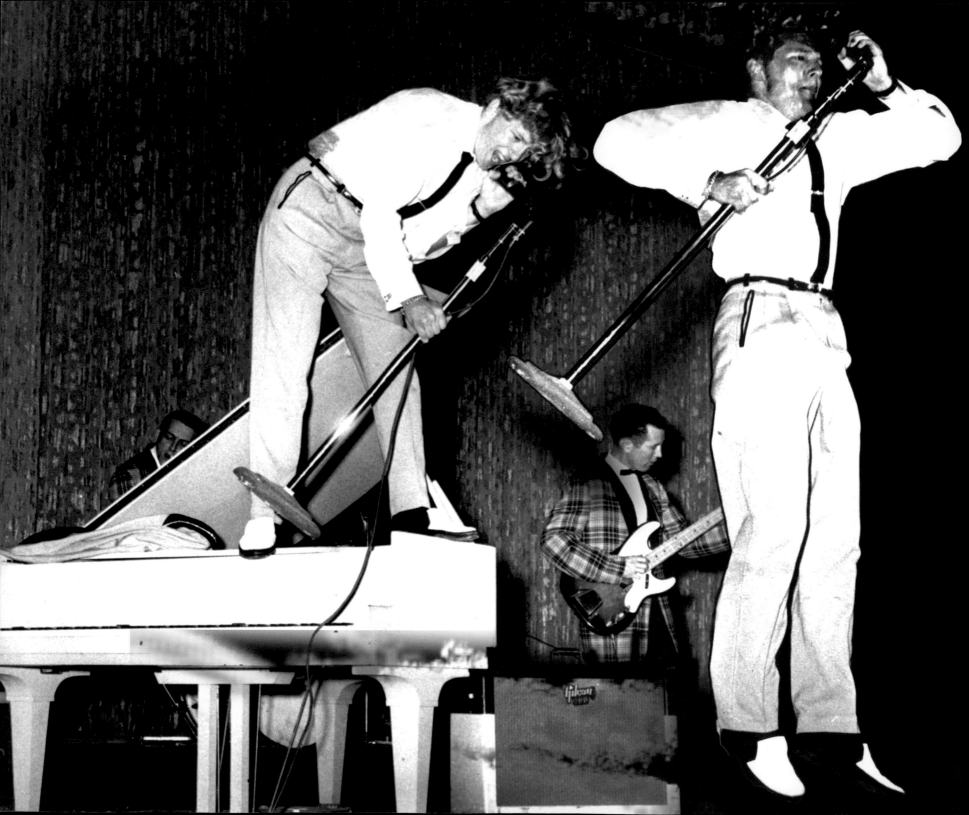

TO ROCK OR NOT TO ROCK

Some in Jerry Lee's family, and most of his school orderlies, considered The Killer incorrigible, even at an early age. A traveling preacher, Brother Barton, had a young and beautiful daughter. One day the pair arrived at the Assembly of God church in Ferriday. Jerry Lee immediately felt attracted to Brother Barton's daughter, Dorothy. The two teenagers quickly became seriously involved, to the point of shame. In an attempt to avoid family scandal, Jerry Lee married Dorothy.

And so in 1950, Jerry Lee's mother shipped off her conflicted and profligate fifteen-year-old son to study the Bible at the Southeastern Assemblies of God University in Waxahachie, Texas. Mother Mamie wanted to avoid further gossip and still harbored great plans for her young prodigy—and she didn't want him to squander his God-given genius on "that show business world." She wanted Jerry Lee to apply his talents and his life to glorifying the Lord. Cousin Jimmy had shown interest in becoming a piano-playing preacher, and Jerry Lee had some aspirations for that same general "calling." Yet soon after arriving in his new surroundings, the maniacal lifestyle of the *real* Jerry Lee Lewis again asserted itself and fixed his destiny.

Selected to play the piano for a church school assembly featuring the best gospel songs, Jerry Lee flew into a (rather natural for him) boogie-woogie rendition of "My God Is Real." The shock of this blasphemy quickly ignited into rage, and with prayer and little else, the ministers-in-charge hastily sent Mr. Lewis back to the farm in Ferriday. This event would widen Jerry Lee's emotional separation from his spiritual roots, and ever after he would feel torn between the worlds of the sacred and the profane. This splitting of calls constantly ate away at him and helped lead to many well-publicized incidents of erratic behavior.

THE MEM

By the time Jerry Lee Lewis stepped inside Sam Phillips's Sun Records in Memphis, he "had been thrown out of Bible college; been a complete failure as a sewing machine salesman; been turned down by most Nashville-based country music record labels and the coveted Louisana Hayride. Jerry Lee had also been married twice; in jail once; and burned with the passion that he was truly the next big thing—an inference to the superstar career of Elvis Presley." So wrote Cub Koda.

Jerry Lee Lewis found his world in a major down-ward spiral. He had broken up with his first wife, Dorothy, and had quickly married Jane Mitcham, also with child—even before the divorce papers from his first marriage were finalized. Straining to make financial ends meet, Jerry Lee struggled with gigs of repetitious playing in the juke joints, at Haney's, and the Wagon Wheel nightclub across the river in Natchez. His rejection at The Louisiana Hayride audition in Shreveport, and even more so the snubs of several record companies in Nashville, did more than humiliate Jerry Lee Lewis's frag-ile psyche—especially when producers repeatedly taunted Jerry Lee to trade in his piano for a guitar.

HIS SUN IS CALLING

Later Jerry Lee could point to only one positive sign during this unrelenting period of rejection: At least he left Nashville with Roy Hull's cowritten song, "Whole Lotta Shakin' Goin' On," which he had picked up during a short performing stint at Hull's after-hours joint, the Musician's Hideaway. When police raided the illegal after-hours drinking spot, Jerry Lee barely escaped jail and dejectedly returned to his daddy's farm to perfect his piano skills—by playing for the farm animals.

By all accounts, Jerry Lee Lewis really liked and felt greatly envious of Elvis Presley's early recordings. As "Heartbreak Hotel" blasted from every radio station in the country, Jerry Lee realized that a man in Memphis had launched Elvis—and he convinced himself that it was his time to be discovered. Lewis recalls the scenario this way:

I seen a picture in Country Song Roundup with a man called Sam C. Phillips who's releasing records on a guy called Elvis Presley, out of Memphis, on Sun Records. Me and my Daddy was out in the field. We were pulling corn, and I said, "Daddy, I think I'm going to Memphis." I was twenty years old then. I said, "I read about this boy called Elvis Presley who is really something else. And Sam Phillips got him started. I think he could get me started, too."

Mamie and Elmo Lewis sold thirty-nine dozen eggs to Nelson's Grocery Store in Ferriday to finance Jerry Lee's trip. And so he left Louisiana to chase fame and fortune in Memphis. Sun Records producer Jack Clement recalled what happened next.

"I was working with Roy Orbison," he said, "when Sally Wilbourn, our girl up front, came back and says, 'There's this guy out here who says he plays piano just like Chet Atkins.' I said, 'Oh, really? I think I'd better hear that.' So, he came back into the studio, sat down at the Spinet, and played 'Wildwood Flower.' And it sounded just like Chet Atkins playing the piano! And he played another thing or two, and I said, 'Do ya sing?' And Lewis snapped back, 'Oh, yeah. I'm a great singer—I love to play and sing.'"

Something about the young man stopped Clement from throwing him out. "I quickly turned the tape recording machine on because he was *different*," Jack recalled. "He started singing this George Jones song called 'Seasons of My Heart.' So I cut that. And then he went right into another George Jones song, a thing called 'Window Up Above.'"

At the time, Jack recalled, country music was in a bad slump. People in Nashville thought it was the end of the world because of the new Rockabilly hits by Elvis Presley, Carl Perkins, and Johnny Cash that Sun Records was producing. Jack let the tape machine run as he asked Jerry Lee, "Where'd you get all this?" Not at all bashful—and very anxious not to let this golden opportunity sour like the one in Nashville—Jerry Lee confidently answered, "Oh, yes! I'm a stylist. I set my own style. I mean, we live so far back in the country in Louisiana, we get the Grand Ole' Opry on Wednesday night—and on a battery radio, at that. I liked Red Foley, but as I grew older, my mind must have broadened a little bit and I learned to love Hank Williams."

Jack then asked Lewis if he knew "Crazy Arms." When Jerry Lee said he knew some of it, Jack laughed and said, "Well, do what you know of it." And so, Jerry ripped into a blues-country version of the song that made Jack Clement stand up and really listen.

"There wasn't anything on it," Jack remembered, "just Jerry Lee playing piano and a little bit of drum. On the Roy Orbison stuff we were recording when Jerry Lee came in, James Van Eaton was playing drums, Billy Riley was playing bass, and Rowland James was playing guitar. Well, when we did 'Crazy Arms,' Riley and Rowland thought we were taking a break. One of them was in the toilet and the other was somewhere else. Jerry Lee just kept singing and the tape was running, so there was nothing on that 'Crazy Arms' recording but Jerry Lee Lewis's piano and Van Eaton's drum—except for the very end when Billy Riley rushed in, picks up the electric guitar, and hits a little bad chord on the end of the song. It was such an amazing one-take performance by Jerry Lee, we just let it stay that way—sort of raw and primitive."

When Sam Phillips heard the crude live demo Jack Clement had cut with Jerry Lee, he loved it. Sam questioned Jack, "Where in the world did he come from? I can hear a lot of spiritual stuff in there. I don't care where he came from, just get him back in here as fast as you can."

Just as Jack phoned Jerry Lee to give him the news, Jerry Lee and his bass player cousin, J. W. Brown, walked into the studio. The timing couldn't have been more perfect. When Jerry Lee and J. W. entered the control room, Sam and Jack were playing "Crazy Arms." Immediately Sam Phillips said to The Killer, "Now, I can sell that!"

Sam coupled "Crazy Arms" with a little song Jerry Lee had written called "End of the Road"—a timely expression of what Jerry Lee Lewis was trying to escape. And with this new Sun Records deal, as they say, The Killer was on his way.

A WHOLE LOTTA SHAKIN' BEGINS

"Crazy Arms" sold about 140,000 copies—excellent for a cover of a song that was already a hit by Ray Price on the country charts. So immediately the brain trust at Sun Records went to work on a follow-up.

Jack Clement had written a song called "It'll Be Me," and Jerry Lee and his band started working on an arrangement for it. During a short pause in the action, Jerry Lee's bass player, J. W. Brown, said, "Hey, Jerry Lee, do that song that we've been doing on the shows that everybody likes so much." Jack had taken a short break and was standing in the studio near the control room door. He quickly ran back into the control room and hit the play and record buttons on the monoral Ampex recorder. He sat down at the board just as Jerry Lee ripped into "Whole Lotta Shakin' Goin' On."

"I mean, no rundown, no dry run, nothing—just pure, raw Jerry Lee Lewis, pounding and romping all over that piano and singing that song like he was possessed," Jack recalled. "I had the mic levels set for the other song, but it didn't matter. It was recording on the fly—what I heard is what I got, and that was it. One take."

In the middle of the song, Jerry Lee forgot some of Roy Hull's original lyrics, so he just eased the band down, kept the piano rhythm pounding and started talking, just like he was onstage and working the audience. It was amazing—and very suggestive. Suddenly, he roared back up for a powerful and triumphant finish.

Sam Phillips liked the song and loved Jerry's performance, but worried that it might be a bit too suggestive for the radio stations. After all, rock and roll was still in its infancy and other recordings with even *slight* sexual suggestion had been banned in critical sales markets like Boston. Sam's good friend Dewey Phillips felt otherwise. He felt as strong about "Shakin'" as he had on "That's All Right (Mama)" and "Blue Suede Shoes." He played it over and over—and within a week, it was well on its way to the top of the local Memphis radio playlist charts.

Sam finally put everything he had behind "Whole Lotta Shakin'" and sent his brother, Judd Phillips, to New York with Jerry Lee in search of a national television shot. Jerry Lee said of this trip, "Sam gave us five hundred dollars to go to New York and back home, and Judd spent most of it in a bar before we got out of the New York airport. We went downtown and Ed Sullivan closed the door in our face; but Jules Green, Steve Allen's manager, listened to me play 'Whole Lotta Shakin'' and immediately gave us one thousand dollars to hold us over so Steve Allen could hear me play the next day. The next day Steve Allen walked into the studio and sat down; I took my bubble gum out of my mouth and popped it up on the piano and laid into 'Whole Lotta Shakin'.' Mr. Allen said, 'I want this boy on my show this Sunday night.' And that was that!"

Jerry Lee Lewis's debut television performance on *The Steve Allen Show*, July 28, 1957, firmly placed The Killer into rock and roll history. It is said that Jerry Lee Lewis's performance that night was "nothing short of demonic." It sent the record to the top of the country and rhythm and blues charts; and only Debbie Reynolds's "Tammy" kept Jerry Lee out of the number one position in the *Billboard* pop charts, where he settled for number two. The record sold over two million copies and entrenched Jerry Lee Lewis into that long-awaited superstardom arena he had dreamed of for years.

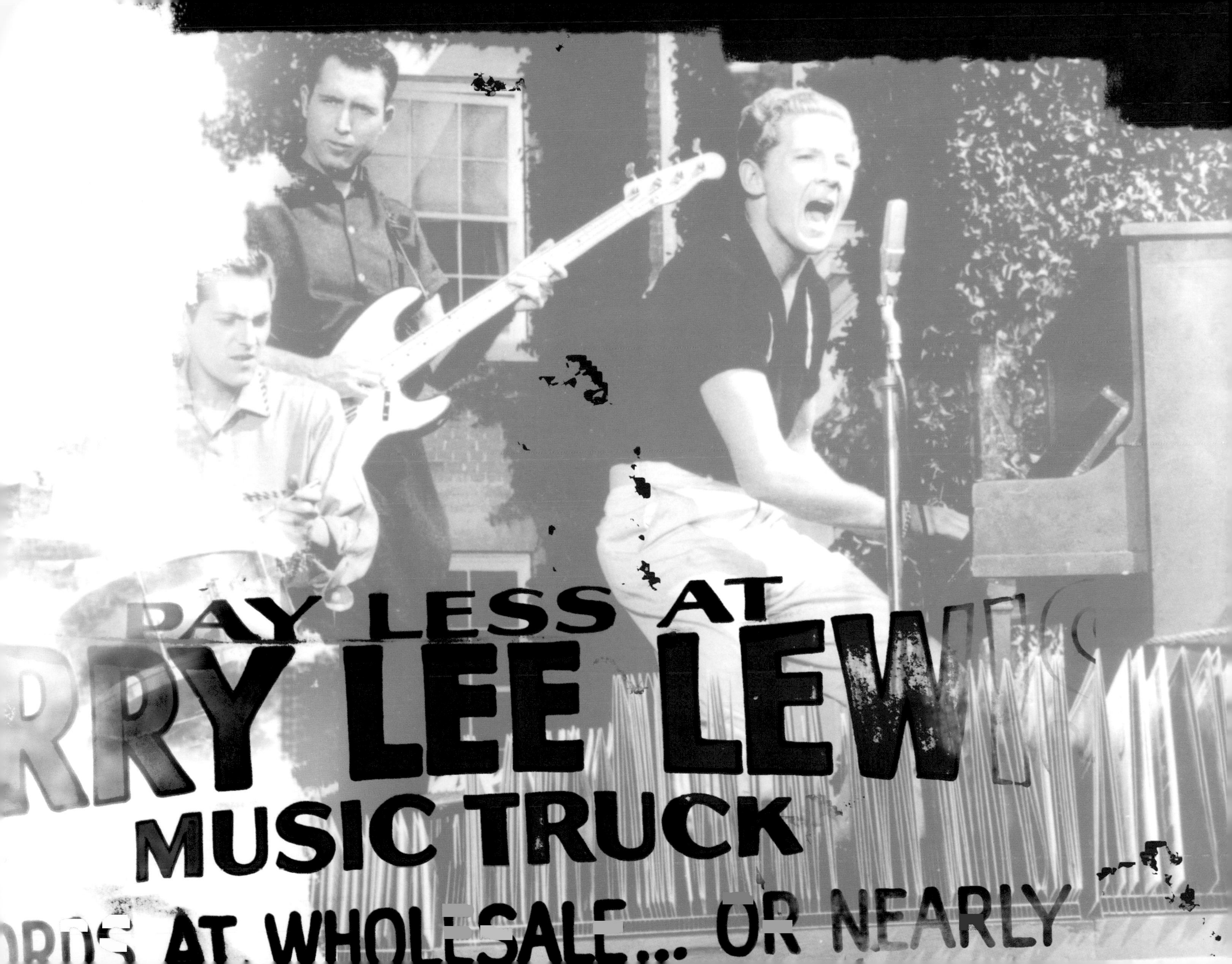
PAY LESS AT
RRY LEE LEW
MUSIC TRUCK
AT WHOLESALE... OR NEARLY

THE GREAT BALL of FIRE

Jerry Lee Lewis

MEAN WOMAN BLUES

I'M FEELIN' SORRY

WHOLE LOT OF SHAKIN' GOIN' ON

TURN AROUND

Hi Lo Music, Inc.
BMI

U-29
Vocal
2:11

DOWN THE LINE
(Orbison)
JERRY LEE LEWIS
And His Pumping Piano
288

RECORD COMPANY

MEMPHIS, TENNESSEE

SUN
RECORD COMPANY

Marlyn Music
BMI U-247

Vocal

WHOLE LOT OF SHAKIN' GOING ON
(D. Williams — S. David)
JERRY LEE LEWIS
267

MEMPHIS, TENNESSEE

SUN

BRS Music Co.
BMI

GREAT BALLS OF FIRE
(Hammer-Blackwell)
JERRY LEE LEWIS
And His Pumping Piano
281

MEMPHIS, TENNESSEE

JAMBOREE TO THE TOP

IN AUGUST 1957, JERRY LEE WAS SIGNED TO PERFORM IN THE ROCK STAR-FILLED MOVIE *JAMBOREE*, WHICH ALSO STARRED FATS DOMINO AND CARL PERKINS, AMONG OTHERS. OTIS BLACKWELL, THE MOVIE'S MUSICAL DIRECTOR, ASSIGNED "GREAT BALLS OF FIRE"—A NEW SONG IN WHICH HE HAD A FIFTY PERCENT SHARE OF OWNERSHIP—TO JERRY LEE FOR HIS DEBUT MOVIE PERFORMANCE.

THE MOVIE BECAME A BOX OFFICE SUCCESS, AND BY THAT DECEMBER, "GREAT BALLS OF FIRE" WAS SITTING AT NUMBER ONE ON ALL THREE OF THE NATIONAL CHARTS—COUNTRY, POP, AND RHYTHM AND BLUES.

SUDDENLY, JERRY LEE LEWIS HAD BECOME THE HOTTEST PHENOMENON IN FIFTIES ROCK AND ROLL.

SECOND COUSINS, TWICE REMOVED

Jerry Lee Lewis celebrated his new stardom by running off to Hernando, Mississippi, with the barely teenaged daughter of his cousin, J. W. Brown. There, twenty-two-year-old Jerry Lee Lewis and his thirteen-year-old second cousin, Myra Gale Brown, were secretly married in a civil ceremony.

On May 23, 1958, Jerry Lee Lewis, his sister Frankie, and his third wife, Myra, arrived in London, England, to begin a short tour. The British press caught wind of Myra's tender age and began a tabloid rampage that promptly caused the cancellation of the tour and this trip to be cut short.

Jerry Lee's second hit, "Great Balls of Fire," carved The Killer's place well into music history. This, his biggest hit, made him a household name in most countries of the world. His 1958 follow-up, "Breathless" and "High School Confidential," continued his chart-topping journey in both the U.S. and the U.K. In all, Sun Records wound up with four monster hits from Jerry Lee Lewis in just twenty-four months. Elvis was serving in the army at the time, and Jerry Lee basked in the success of his four huge hits.

"The word was he was going to replace Elvis as being the most popular," remembers Bill Griggs.

THE PACE SLOWS

Nothing reasonable seemed able to stop this one man piano-wrecking superstar performer—but maybe one *un*reasonable thing could slow down his breakneck pace.

Back in the United States, Jerry Lee Lewis stared career-ending problems straight in the face when major U.S. papers and radio stations picked up the British story of The Killer's marriage to his thirteen-year-old second cousin. Many radio stations banned Jerry Lee Lewis's recordings, and even his most ardent followers began abandoning him.

Even so, Jerry Lee's version of Ray Charles's "What'd I Say" found new success in the pop music charts by 1961. A brilliant version of "Chantilly Lace" followed. This opened the door for a pivotal return for The Killer. In May of 1962, with the help of television producer friend Jack Good, Jerry Lee Lewis made a triumphant reentry into England. The following April, The Killer returned once more to England to set box office records, reestablish his good name and regain his superstar reign over rock and roll.

In July 1969, Shelby Singleton signed Jerry Lee Lewis to a lucrative recording contract with Mercury Records—and thus began a long and solid string of top ten country music hits for one of the most complicated and loved superstar artists of our time.

INTO THE HALL OF FAME

Jack Clement said of The Killer, "I'll tell you the magic of Jerry Lee, the reason he was so good. He'd go in the studio and perform just like he does on the stage. You give him an audience of one or two people, and he gives you the whole show."

The Killer gave us some great music, and that's why he will forever be included among the royalty of fifties rock and roll, a true Rockabilly Legend. Along with Elvis Presley and Buddy Holly, Jerry Lee Lewis was inducted into the Rock and Roll Hall of Fame and Museum in 1986, an honored member of the very first class.

I will always keep Jerry Lee Lewis in my closely held list of those I most admire and appreciate. But most of all, I will remember those incredible days and nights we performed together in two to three hour, nonstop mega-medley shows—performances we could never repeat. Those are the terrific days I have comfortably stored away in my mental sound studio and photo gallery.

I can't help but agree wholeheartedly with George Hunt, who said, "There's a lot of vibrancy in Jerry Lee, an amazing amount of energy—let's call it *spontaneous combustion!*"

BUDDY

JOHNNY HORTON

BOB LUMAN

JOHNNY & DORSEY BURNETTE

FELLAS, WE HARDLY KNEW YE

CAN YOU IMAGINE PERFORMING ON THE SAME BILL AS ELVIS PRESLEY, BUDDY HOLLY, ROY ORBISON, CARL PERKINS, JOHNNY CASH, BUDDY KNOX, CHARLIE RICH, JERRY LEE LEWIS, JOHNNY HORTON, BOB LUMAN, GENE VINCENT, AND DORSEY AND JOHNNY BURNETTE?

WHILE NEVER ONCE DID ALL OF THESE LEGENDS PERFORM ON THE SAME STAGE AT THE SAME TIME, I CERTAINLY HAVE FIRSTHAND KNOWLEDGE OF HOW IT FELT TO PERFORM WITH MOST OF THEM.

AND THAT'S WHY IT HURTS SO MUCH TO HAVE LOST SO MANY OF THEM SO EARLY.

On the bleak Saturday morning of November 5, 1960, my phone rang. I heard the quivering voice of Johnny Rivers, a native of Shreveport and close friend of Johnny Horton's wife, Billy Jean, say to me, "Jerry, Johnny is dead. He was killed in a head-on collision last night in Texas."

I found the message almost impossible to grasp. It brought back all the hurt I had felt with the deaths of Buddy Holly, J. P. Richardson ("The Big Bopper") and Ritchie Valens. I felt guilty and terribly frightened—guilty that I was about to become the new lead singer of the Crickets as a result of Buddy's untimely death, and frightened as to what might be in store for me. I think many of us in those days felt the immense impact of how closely death stalks us all.

Only a month later, while crisscrossing the nation to visit disc jockeys and radio station program directors in the major American markets, I booked a flight to New York City from Washington D. C. For no reason at all, save the news of a major snowstorm in New York, I changed my schedule and instead purchased a new ticket to Miami, where I was to be the following Tuesday. As I arrived at the Miami International Airport, I got the shocking news that the original flight I had booked had collided with another aircraft over New York City. No one survived.

You don't understand or forget experiences like these. Losing your friends in airplane and auto accidents—and knowing the deep vacancy of such a loss—layers the pain that stays with you forever.

Still, you continue to work every day and night. Weary from lack of sleep and exhausted from shows that went on too long, and with emotions raw as red meat, you travel thousands of miles per year to the next show, under all imaginable conditions and on various conveyances. And when the next show ends and you find yourself bottomed-out and all alone at an unknown hotel room in some unknown city, you remember those who have died . . . and fear of your own destiny overcomes you. Yet the next morning, you awake with a mixture of anxiety and heightened adrenaline both kicking you in the butt to again, somehow, find your place onstage.

There is no way to explain how close the bonds of friendship grow between those of us who worked together on the road in the early days. Likewise, there is no way to aptly express our feelings of loss for those who are now gone. You hear their music. You see their records in the shops . . . and you wonder—*What would it have been like if all of us could have grown old together? How would our world have changed?*

While there's no way to answer that question, one thing, at least, is for sure. Our world certainly *did* change by having the following Legends in it, even if only for far too short a time.

HORTON is considered by sporting goods rs as one of the best fresh water fisher-ever cast an artificial lure. Johnny has many prize winning bass out of lakes are hard to catch. Now in the entertain-, JOHNNY HORTON is reeling in some esting records with reactions equal to a . All of the records listed here are striking g catches and you'll feel them weighing the contest line.

IE CHECKERS PLAYER

Tillman Franks grew up in a world of honky-tonks and hillbilly music—that triangle between Louisiana, Texas, and Arkansas that he called "The Country Soul of the World." Franks, a slap-bass playing personal manager to a lot of the country acts on The Louisiana Hayride, saw the gold at the Rockabilly rainbow and pushed one of these acts to join the freight.

Johnny Horton had the unique vocal styling, the looks, and the rhythm to compete with Elvis, Perkins, and Cash. He just needed Tillman's special firecracker stimulation to move from the middle of the pack to the top.

Johnny showed up at Tillman's door on Summer Street one day, rang the bell, and said, "Tillman, I know you're not working, but if you'll manage me, I'll get to number one."

"I don't like to hear you sing," Tillman replied.

"That's no problem," Johnny answered, "I'll sing any way you want me to." And that's how the two got together.

Johnny and Tillman made a great team as artist and manager. They both were very intelligent and knew how to get things done.

After Elvis, all the big record companies wanted a Rockabilly act, and Columbia was no exception. One day its executives asked Johnny and Tillman to visit Bradley's Barn recording studio in Nashville. The still-broke duo sold a couple of songs and borrowed a car to make the trip from Shreveport. As Tillman turned the dial on the radio, all he could hear was Elvis Presley. He snapped it off and said nothing for a few moments. Finally Johnny asked, "Chief, what are you thinking about?"

"He's nothing but a monster," Tillman replied.

"Who's a monster?" Johnny asked.

"Elvis Presley is a monster. He's about all you hear on the radio." Tillman paused and then said firmly, "I'm going to build me a monster."

"Who's going to be your monster?" Johnny wondered.

"You are," Tillman answered.

Arriving in Memphis practically on fumes—some 175 miles short of Nashville—Johnny and Tillman stopped by Elvis's new house to ask for a small loan. Elvis saw them coming and ran all the way down the driveway. He hugged Johnny and said, "I get so lonesome to see somebody, even though all those kids are screaming out there in the street."

"Elvis," Johnny said after telling him about his recording session, "We come by to borrow ten bucks off of you to get on to Nashville."

Elvis yelped with excitement about Johnny's new session and quickly answered, "Is that all you need?"

Tillman then chimed in, telling Elvis that he felt uncomfortable playing slap bass on Johnny's session—so could they "borrow" Bill Black? Elvis quickly agreed, on one condition: "You can get Bill Black to play on the session, but tell everybody that it was you, Tillman, playing bass." That's how Bill Black joined the others for the trip to Nashville and played slap bass on Johnny's first Columbia session.

The time in Nashville could hardly have gone better. "Honky Tonk Man" came out of it, which Columbia chose for release. It had all the trappings of the new pushy Rockabilly sound. Grady Martin, Nashville's best lead guitar player, put his trademark licks on the record, along with the booming rhythm of Harold Bradley and the Elvis-type slap bass of Bill Black.

When Tillman Franks heard the playback of "Honky Tonk Man," he looked at Johnny and said, "Johnny, you've done it with this one! You're no longer the 'Singing Fisherman,' you're now the 'Honky Tonk Man.'" The record became a distinctive country music and Rockabilly hit. It launched a superstar career for Johnny Horton. "Honky Tonk Man" reached number nine on the country chart and number fourteen on the *Billboard* top-forty pop chart.

To that point, Johnny had been restricted by contract from touring too far away from Tyler, Texas, where he worked every Monday night on television station KLTV. If he was going to tour, he needed to get out of the contract; so one night when he was supposed to read a commercial for Holsum Bread, he said, "Friends, we are proud to be here and proud to be sponsored by Holsum Bread. Tillman Franks, my manager, eats Holsum Bread, and I eat it, too. What I like about Holsum Bread is that it's never touched by hand. That's right, they mix it with their feet." After the show, the station owner released him and he began to travel.

To really understand Johnny Horton, you have to know that he was a good fisherman, and any good fisherman must have a special relationship with his soul. You have to be very gentle, you have to know when to be quiet, you have to know how to study the fish—and Johnny had mastered all of that. He used to say, "There's three things you've got to know about fish. They're either mad, curious, or hungry, and all you've got to do is figure out which one of them they are—and then you've got them." Johnny Horton used his knowledge of fishing in many settings throughout his abbreviated life.

WHEN HE PERFORMED, JOHNNY WOULD OFTEN SING SO HARD THAT THE BLOOD VESSELS IN HIS NECK POPPED OUT. HE GAVE IT EVERYTHING HE HAD . . . USUALLY. BUT SOMETIMES, HIS LOVE OF FISHING GOT IN THE WAY. ON SOME NIGHTS HE STARTED THINKING OF LANDING A BIG ONE, AND HIS PERFORMING INTENSITY WOULD DROP. TILLMAN ALWAYS NOTICED AND WOULD WHISPER TO HIM, "I MEAN TO SING IT, JOHNNY." HE'D STEP UP IN HIS FACE AND TELL HIS FRIEND, "WHEN I SAY SING, I MEAN SING!" AND JOHNNY WOULD ALWAYS RESPOND. HE LIKED TILLMAN TO PUSH HIM LIKE THAT; THEY WERE NOT JUST MANAGER AND SINGER, BUT CLOSE FRIENDS.

And that's why the loss of Johnny Horton devastated everyone in the Rockabilly world—but especially wounded Tillman.

"Well, I loved him," Tillman remembers with tears. "I wasn't just his manager. We were partners."

Not long before Johnny passed away, he began having premonitions of his death. He started telling friends and family that he would soon die at the hands of a drunk. And on November 5, 1960, after a gig at the Skyline Club in Austin, Texas, it happened. While driving home to Shreveport after the performance, an intoxicated nineteen-year-old drove his truck straight into Johnny's car as the vehicles crossed a bridge. The accident occurred about 2 a.m. near Milano, Texas.

"He was driving when he was killed, and I was in the front seat," Tillman remembers. "My head was lying against his shoulder. He always told me that he was going to take care of me, and he has. His records are doing better than ever."

At the funeral, Tillman felt a strong urge to shake his deceased friend's hand. He couldn't, of course, but he and Johnny always shook hands just before going onstage; that was their ritual. Immediately after a performance, they shook hands again. Since Tillman considered the funeral Johnny's final performance, he longed to shake his hand one last time.

Another friend who took the loss especially hard was Johnny Cash. "I don't guess there's ever been a death of a family member that affected or hurt Johnny Cash any worse than the loss of his best friend, Johnny Horton," reflected W. S. Holland. "Johnny Cash idolized Johnny Horton, and his death really upset him." Cash flew in to Shreveport for the funeral on a chartered airplane and read chapter 20 from the New Testament book of John.

"I DON'T GUESS THERE'S EVER BEEN A DEATH OF A FAMILY MEMBER THAT AFFECTED OR HURT JOHNNY CASH ANY WORSE THAN THE LOSS OF HIS BEST FRIEND, JOHNNY HORTON. JOHNNY CASH IDOLIZED JOHNNY HORTON, AND HIS DEATH REALLY UPSET HIM."

– W. S. HOLLAND, DRUMMER FOR CARL PERKINS AND JOHNNY CASH

Johnny Cash and Johnny Horton

For my own part, I can honestly say that I never met a nicer person in the entertainment world than Johnny Horton. You can call him "The Honky Tonk Man," "The Singing Fisherman," or just "Johnny," but I'll always call him "gentleman" and "friend."

Tillman still misses the dear friend he lost so long ago. He remembers not only the musician and the fisherman, but the checkers player. The two used to play checkers all the time.

"We had a bet one time that if Johnny beat me three straight games, he'd pull his britches down and I'd have to kiss his bare behind," Tillman recalls. "He got two games—and I had a nervous breakdown and went home."

He laughs, and for a moment the pain feels a little less sharp.

Johnny Gale Horton: April 30, 1925 — November 5, 1960

THE NEXT BEST THING TO ELVIS HIMSELF

In September 1955, Gene Vincent had just been released from the navy and was recovering from a serious motorcycle accident in which he almost lost his left leg. He hobbled into Hank Snow's All Star Jamboree show in Norfolk, Virginia, Gene's hometown. The show featured Cowboy Copus, the Louvin Brothers (Ira and Charlie), and Jimmie Rodgers. As an added attraction to the bill, WCMS Radio had added the new Rockabilly sensation, Elvis Presley—along with Scotty Moore and Bill Black.

As with each of us before him, Gene's life changed the moment he saw Elvis Presley perform.

I first met Gene Vincent in San Angelo, Texas, in early 1956. He played Gwen Field Baseball Park, our little Tom Green County baseball stadium. My pals—Toby Yeager, Bobby Young, Leon Davidson, and I—had a little Rockabilly group, and we opened the show. We thought we'd kicked pretty good. The live performance of our regional recording "Hillbilly Bop" thrilled our young lady-fans as they danced around and screamed for us.

And then Gene Vincent and his Blue Caps band stormed onstage with a tough-guy disposition that would cause the boldest to shrink. Now, I'd witnessed Elvis in 1955 and thought *that* was the greatest performance I'd ever seen. But when Gene hit the stage, it was as if he took everything Elvis had done and moved it up by several degrees. Gene Vincent was an astonishing experience in time.

With his withered, braced leg, this amazing singer/performer hit that outdoor stage like a West Texas tornado. His movements and singing were over the top, and his musicians blew me away. They were pushing Gene right up to the edge of everything and then competing against him for the exaggerated extreme. It was explosive stuff!

Cliff Gallop's faster-than-lightning guitar leads stunned all of us. Then there was "Wee" Willie Williams on rhythm guitar, "Jumpin'" Jack Neal on upright string bass, and fifteen-year-old Dickie "Be-Bop" Harrell on drums. What a group! These same musicians played on all the early hit records, and their live performance stayed right in your face, all the way. So it shouldn't surprise anyone that, decades later, *Rolling Stone* magazine would declare that Gene Vincent and The Blue Caps were America's first rock and roll band.

Gene Vincent gave a new, dynamic definition to Rockabilly—and right there in the public arena of my hometown, Vincent unquestionably introduced primal sex into Rockabilly. West Texas had never seen anything like him.

While everybody's favorite subject at the time was the "Elvis Presley shake," few people realized that this shaking originated purely by accident. Elvis was scared to death during his first live performance at the Memphis Overton Shell amphitheater and during "That's All Right (Mama)," Elvis's legs shook uncontrollably. The more he tried to calm down, the more they shook—and the girls went crazy over it. That's how it all began.

BUDDY HOLLY LIKED GENE VINCENT. AND BUDDY KINDA
SOUNDS LIKE GENE VINCENT ON SOME OF HIS SONGS
THAT HE RECORDED.

— JERRY COLEMAN, ROCKABILLY DJ, KDAV RADIO, LUBBOCK, TEXAS

BUT GENE VINCENT WASN'T SCARED. HE WASN'T FRIGHTENED OF ANYTHING. HE WASN'T SHAKING; HE WAS AGGRESSIVE, AND IT'S THAT AGGRESSIVENESS YOU HEARD IN HIS MUSIC AND SAW IN HIS STAGE PERFORMANCE.

Gene Vincent plunged into all-out Rockabilly, equally capable of fast-paced exuberance and whispery, sensitive vocal expression. Ironically, Gene also was the first to use that little "hiccup" in his singing, something both Buddy Holly and I later adopted and developed. You can hear it in several phrases of his biggest hit, "Be-Bop-a-Lula."

Gene was born Vincent Eugene Craddock on February 11, 1935, and came from the same kind of economically challenged, post-Depression rural background as the rest of us. He taught himself to play guitar and often performed with neighborhood black musicians on the porch of his parents' country store. With the permission of his father, he dropped out of high school at age seventeen and joined the navy.

Three years later, Gene was riding a brand-new Triumph motorcycle when he collided with a car and broke his left shinbone. He failed to allow the broken leg to heal properly and almost lost it to amputation. Doctors fitted him with a metal brace in 1957 that he wore for the rest of his life. Yet his injured leg never stopped him from pulling out all the stops on stage.

A show promoter once told Carl Perkins, "I've got a boy to open for you. Watch him perform and tell me what you think."

Carl heard Gene sing, "Be-Bop-a-Lula, a she's my baa-by," and immediately Perkins said, "Aha! I think it's a hit song." And he was exactly right. Years later Carl remembered, "I knew he was not only going to have a hit record, but Gene Vincent was going to have a career. He was doing what Elvis was doing, what I was trying to do, and doing it better."

He was doing it better because he had something freer about him, something more reckless, wild, lusty—and add to that his outlaw look, with signature T-shirt, blue jeans, greasy hair and black leathers. Gene Vincent was an original rocker with a bad boy image.

By early 1956, Gene cut some demo recordings while appearing on the WCMS radio station with a group called The Virginians. Local disc jockey "Sheriff" Tex Davis signed Gene to a personal management contract and got the demo tape to Ken Nelson, a prominent staff producer for Capitol Records in Nashville.

Capitol, like the other major labels, wanted its own version of Elvis to compete against RCA, so Nelson agreed to record four sides with Gene. On May 4, 1956, Gene Vincent and The Blue Caps arrived at the historic Bradley's Barn Recording Studio for its first session. Ken Nelson felt unsure about the performance abilities of Gene's band members, so he had gathered Nashville's best studio musicians—including Grady Martin on lead guitar, Hank "Sugar Foot" Garland on guitar, Buddy Harman on piano, and Bob Moore on bass.

In Buddy Holly style, Gene insisted that he audition the songs with his own band; and Nelson, unlike Owen Bradley in his confrontation with Buddy Holly, agreed.

When Cliff Gallop ripped into the lead intro of "Race with the Devil," Nashville's best beat a hasty retreat from the studio. Can you imagine such legendary studio musicians as Grady Martin, Hank Garland, and Bob Moore becoming intimidated by these young, unknown Virginia musicians? They are reported to have said simply to Ken Nelson, "No improvements can be made on that picking," and they all left the barn.

Gene was among the first early rock pioneers to record with his own band, joining the legendary Rockabilly artists with Sun Records, along with Buddy Knox and Buddy Holly at Norman Petty's studio. This was one of the things that made Rockabilly stand out—the performance just couldn't be "too perfect" or it wouldn't work. It had to be freer and come from the heart; the performers had to feel it. And these guys really felt it!

"Be-Bop-a-Lula" was first up to be recorded, and Ken Nelson, new to Rockabilly and trying to mimic Sam Phillips's magical slap-back echo sound, had the engineer, Mort Thomasson, crank up the tape delay echo to an exaggerated point to enhance Gene Vincent's singing.

The mystery is that it really worked! It worked so well, in fact, that within twenty-eight days of the record's release on June 2, 1956, it sold over two hundred thousand copies. "Be-Bop-a-Lula" stayed at the top of the national pop and country charts until October 1956—an unprecedented twenty weeks—and sold more than one million copies, the fastest-selling of any of the fifties rock and roll/Rockabilly million-selling records.

Even today there's a little controversy over where "Be-Bop-a-Lula" came from. One story says that Don Graves, a fellow patient at the hospital where Gene recovered after his motorcycle accident, wrote "Be-Bop-a-Lula" as an ode to a local stripper and that Gene paid him fifty dollars for the rights to it. Another account says that Gene and "Sheriff" Tex Davis wrote the song together one afternoon while listening to a 78 RPM recording of "You Can Bring Pearl with the Turned-Up Nose, But Don't Bring Lulu." Yet another says Gene and Don Graves wrote it together, based on a comic strip heroine named Little Lulu and that Tex later bought Don's rights to the song for twenty-five dollars.

Which story is accurate? Since Gene is no longer around to set the record straight, we'll probably never know.

What is certain is that out of Gene's first recording session also came "Race with the Devil," "Woman Love," and "I Sure Miss You." To capitalize on the band's success, Ken Nelson had the boys back in the studio in late June for a four-day recording session. They cut sixteen tracks during this marathon recording session, including "Blue Jean Bop," which went gold.

In 1956, before Gene got his brace, he sang in the movie *Woman Love*. Producers hid his cast under his jeans and painted the toe of the cast to look like a shoe.

The British creative genius, music television host and producer Jack Good provided Gene Vincent with an appropriate image as the original "rock and roll rebel." Writer Richard Unterberger poetically memoralized Jack Good's iconic Gene Vincent creation like this: "The leather-clad, limping, greasy-haired singer was also one of Rockabilly's original bad boys, lionized by romanticists of past and present generations attracted to his primitive, sometimes savage style and indomitable spirit."

Gene Vincent toured England and Europe and flourished there. In fact, he and Buddy Holly are often cited as the two greatest American influences on the British Invasion that would soon sweep the world—even more important than Elvis Presley or Johnny Cash. Gene wielded such massive impact because of his extraordinary stage performances, many times replicated by the likes of Mick Jagger, among others.

In 1957 Gene appeared on *American Bandstand* and toured Australia with Little Richard and Eddie Cochran; Eddie and he soon became close friends. In November of that year Gene also appeared on *The Ed Sullivan Show*, but by this time pain from his leg injury was driving him to drink heavily; some report that he was also regularly taking two bottles of aspirin at a time to ease his suffering.

In December of 1959, Gene visited England again and received something close to a hero's welcome. He convinced Eddie Cochran to join him for a twelve-week tour, but tragedy overtook the friends on April 17, 1960. Gene and Eddie and Eddie's girlfriend, Sharon Sheeley, were riding in a taxicab when about 1 a.m., the vehicle rounded a curve and hit a cement post at a speed estimated to be about seventy miles per hour. The impact threw Eddie from the cab and killed him.

"When the three of us traveled together," Gene later said, "Sharon always sat in the middle. But because of the crowd of fans at the venue, I got in the cab first, then Eddie, then Sharon last. With Eddie in the middle, the only way he could have flown out that door was if he tried to cover Sharon. The only way I came out alive was because I had taken a sleeping pill. After the crash, I woke up and carried Eddie over to the ambulance, even though I had a broken arm. I was in such a state of shock that I thought nothing was wrong with me. Eddie died two days later on Easter Sunday. Somehow, I didn't."

Gene never again enjoyed the kind of commercial success he had achieved with "Be-Bop-a-Lula" and "Blue Jean Bop," and his health declined steadily over the next several years. He died on October 12, 1971, of a bleeding ulcer. He was just thirty-six years old.

When I think of Gene Vincent, I fondly remember the vibrant, very much alive fireball of a performer I first saw in San Angelo, Texas, back in 1956. And I recall that when "Be-Bop-a-Lula" was first released, even Elvis's own mother thought she heard her son on the record!

I guess there's really no way to compare Gene Vincent with Elvis Presley or anyone else. His individuality stands soundly on its own. And his honored place in fifties rock and roll/Rockabilly history remains forever assured.

On January 12, 1998, Gene Vincent was inducted into the Rock and Roll Hall of Fame and Museum at the thirteenth annual induction dinner. John Fogerty was his presenter.

Vincent Eugene Craddock: February 11, 1935 – October 12, 1971

THE FIRST MILLION SELLER IN WEST TEXAS

What kind of a return could one possibly get from a sixty-dollar, high-risk cash investment in 1956? Well, in one particular situation, the return was *monumental*!

How about the massive return of two phonograph recordings that became all-time classic rock and roll standards that sold over fifteen million copies worldwide? Add to that the building of a superstar career for a young West Texas singer-songwriter who recorded two more million-selling gold records within the next year—a national and international entertainment accomplishment that paved the road for at least two other mega-superstar recording artists to visit the same recording studio and change the world of music forever. So the result of this unique sixty-buck investment must be, by all financial standards, one of the most lucrative investments ever made—and made by guys, as both Buddy Knox and Donnie Lanier confessed, who had "no idea what we were doing."

Buddy Knox, Donnie Lanier, and Jimmy Bowen—West Texans known as the Rhythm Orchids—paved the road to superstardom for Buddy Holly and The Crickets, Roy Orbison, and other fifties rock and roll/Rockabilly artists. The Rhythm Orchids spent sixty dollars for a makeshift vanity recording session at Norman Petty's recording studio, which helped lay a platinum foundation for fifties rock and roll. Multiple million-selling recordings came from this most unusual session—or *sessions*, as it turns out.

The musicians and even some of the instruments were not up to professional standards. The studio, while operated by a professional musician and producer who already had sold over half a million records with a top-charted pop recording, was not actually a "commercial recording facility" at the time of this risky recording. In fact, the owner-producer of the studio didn't much like this new fifties rock and roll/Rockabilly music and admitted to knowing little or nothing about recording it. He even felt the new genre of music to be something of a threat to the smooth pop "cocktail" music that had brought some success to him and his own trio.

THERE'S GOT TO BE A REALLY GOOD STORY HERE

Buddy Knox grew up in Happy, Texas—population seven hundred—a most appropriate hometown for this extraordinarily happy friend.

Buddy Wayne Knox was born on a farm July 20, 1933. Like so many of us, Buddy learned much about music from his mother. Gladys Knox was an amateur musician and singer who performed with her parents and siblings on a gospel music radio show broadcast on a local radio station.

Buddy Knox, like other pioneers of the Rockabilly revolution, was greatly influenced by hillbilly giants he listened to nightly on the family radio: Hank Williams, Jimmie Rodgers, Eddy Arnold, The Carter Family, and Bill Monroe and the Bluegrass Boys.

Buddy's childhood hands were made for a guitar. Buddy told how he learned to play the guitar through the efforts of his mother's sister: "My aunt played guitar really good and sang like a bird. She taught me to play guitar chords. I was just a kid at the time and the strings hurt my fingers, so I figured out a different way to play. I'd tune the guitar to an open G, and I'd bar the chords with my fingers pressed straight across the neck of the guitar, just like Don Everly and Bo Diddley did later. I didn't know many songs, so I started making them up out of my head. I wrote 'Party Doll' and 'Hula Love' when I was about twelve or thirteen years old—around 1948."

Buddy Knox, Donnie Lanier, and Jimmy Bowen originally played in a band called The Serenaders. But the first time they saw Elvis in 1955, their life changed. *Now* they weren't the Serenaders anymore; now they were Rockabilly stars. Elvis changed everything for them.

While attending West Texas State University to earn a degree in psychology and business administration, Buddy and his two friends transformed themselves into a Rockabilly group called the Rhythm Orchids, so called because they all wore orchid-colored shirts. Jimmy Bowen played bass, Donnie Lanier played lead guitar, and Buddy Knox played rhythm guitar and sang.

There is a great story, perhaps fictional, that goes like this:

One night while the Rhythm Orchids were playing for a local college dance, a young stranger named Don Mills climbed up out of the audience, armed with a pair of brushes, and proceeded to play "drums" on a cardboard box, to the amazement of the somewhat irritated Rhythm Orchids. All of a sudden, the dance floor was full of people dancing because of the added push of the drums—or in this case, cardboard shipping box.

Perhaps this was a dream, for Buddy and the boys always seemed to be looking for a good drummer. In a 2006 interview, Rhythm Orchids' guitarist Donnie Lanier claimed no knowledge of this incident and no memory of a drummer named Don Mills.

The Rhythm Orchids played college dances, used car lot openings, drive-in movie theaters, and even performed in local honky-tonks for beer and food, until the management threw them out for being underage. Their original songs were fun and infectious. Buddy's version of "Party Doll" became their most requested number and laid the foundation for one of the biggest success stories in fifties rock and roll/Rockabilly.

The local fans of the Rhythm Orchids loved the band's original music and constantly requested its recordings. One night, Buddy and the band were booked on a West Texas State College frat night show with Roy Orbison and The Teen Kings, and Knox asked Roy where they could record some of their songs to sell to the locals. Orbison told Buddy that he had just cut "Ooby Dooby" at Norman Petty's home studio in Clovis, New Mexico. Roy told Buddy how Norman and his wife, Vi, recorded and performed as the Norman Petty Trio and that the group had sold over a half million records with their release of the popular song "Mood Indigo."

This news intrigued Buddy and his performing pals. They pooled their money and came up with sixty dollars, plus a little extra to pay for the gas to make the drive to New Mexico. Not really sure what the sixty dollars would buy at the studio, the boys strapped the big bass fiddle on top of their car and headed for Clovis.

Buddy laughed as he told of the many surprises they encountered at the recording studio: "Norman Petty and Roy Orbison had failed to tell us that the studio was located on a busy state highway, with noisy trucks constantly rumbling past the building. Without soundproof rooms, the truck noise would show up on the recordings." To get around that problem, the Rhythm Orchids would have to record after the truck traffic stopped, and that happened around midnight to dawn—so the boys slept all day and recorded all night.

Donnie Lanier explained, "In this very first recording attempt at Norman Petty's studio, we were very naïve. We landed there with a lot of hope and little else. We didn't even have a drummer; just Bowen on slap bass, Buddy on rhythm guitar, and me on lead guitar. We only had two songs and Buddy's version of 'Party Doll' had at least *fourteen* verses—sort of a folk song story feel. It was *way* too long. Bowen and I sat down in the studio with Buddy, and we began to cut out most of the verses. Buddy complained, 'Now the song is too short!' and I said, 'Okay, I'll just play two long guitar leads!'"

Donnie remembers that when the Orchids first started recording "Party Doll" with Buddy singing, Norman Petty quickly realized that the band was far from prepared to seriously record. The boys had no drummer, and Jimmy Bowen was really struggling with his slap bass. Buddy was also having a lot of trouble getting comfortable with the revised lyrics and meter of his cut-down song. "After all," Donnie explained, "he'd been singing it with those fourteen verses since he was thirteen."

The boys delegated Jimmy Bowen to be the lead singer for the second song, "I'm Stickin' with You," and this moved along no better than the first ragged 'Party Doll" attempt—if not worse, because Bowen had even more trouble singing and trying to play the slap bass at the same time. All in all, the band's initial attempt at recording was a disaster. Norman suggested that the Orchids go home, regroup—or just plain rehearse—and come back in a week or so.

And that's exactly what they did. Norman Petty set a date for the first part of April 1956—just a few weeks later—and the three Rhythm Orchids headed for home with their tails between their legs.

The trio gathered every personal asset it could muster in preparation for the return to Petty's studio. The boys still had that sixty dollars, and they planned to spend it on making a record or two. Norman was too kind to take any money for the first session and assured the Orchids that the money burning a hole in their pockets would be ample payment for the return recording attempt.

Although the Rhythm Orchids felt wilted, Buddy, Donnie, and Jimmy worked hard on fine-tuning their arrangements of "Party Doll" and "I'm Stickin' with You," even working out some crude arrangements for background vocals. As the day for the trip back to Clovis neared, Buddy got his sister, Verdie, and two of her girlfriends from college to make the trip with them in order to sing background vocals on the session. Donnie Lanier recruited Patricia Everett to play drums. Actually, Donnie was dating her and knew she played the drums pretty badly, but he hoped for a miracle.

Norman Petty felt quite comfortable with "visiting" musicians hanging around the studio on session nights. When this bunch of Rhythm Orchids volunteer supporters arrived, however, he felt a bit unsettled. First of all, the little drummer girl had no set of drums. Her performance gear consisted only of a set of "sock cymbals." In our interview, even Donnie Lanier could not explain the band's plan for a drum kit; all he could remember was what a pretty girl she was—after all, he *was* dating her and she had a very nice set of sock cymbals. The Norman Petty Trio's drummer just happened to be hanging around the studio this midnight evening, and Norman lost no time in recruiting David Alldred to play the drums.

Well, not really the drums, for he didn't have his drums with him. So as if he had planned this substitution, Norman carefully placed a large cardboard shipping box filled with cotton pillows in perfect range of the studio microphones. Truth be known, Norman Petty *preferred* this cardboard box sound over drums because he was not very good at recording the playing of an actual drum kit. So the traveling drummer-in-waiting with the Rhythm Orchids, Pat Everett, was most welcomed to accompany David Alldred's cardboard box drumming with her sock cymbal, and she did so very well.

Pat sat next to David and kept perfect time with her foot, arms, and hands, carefully coordinated to the rhythms determined by Donnie Lanier on the lead guitar. And then Donnie suddenly shouted, "Wait! We haven't figured out a replacement for Jimmy Bowen on the slap bass yet."

Norman Petty vividly remembered Jimmy Bowen's major struggle with his slap bass playing on the previous recording session and immediately began to search for a remedy. Petty's open-door policy at his home studio paid off again when there "just happened" to be a young man hanging out at midnight for the experience of watching the particulars of a recording session. Happily, it turned out that he played acoustic bass fiddle in a college band. So on the spot, Buddy, Jimmy, and Donnie hired the young bass-playing visitor to play Jimmy Bowen's slap bass for the session.

And then another amazing fluke occurred on this all-night recording session. David Bigham and Robert Linville—of The Roses, a popular vocal group from Odessa, Texas, who originally came to Clovis to record "Ooby Dooby" with Roy Orbison—also "just happened" to be hanging out at the studio. Buddy recruited the Roses to join Buddy's sister, Verdie, and Verdie's two friends from college to harmonize background vocals on "Party Doll" and "I'm Stickin' with You."

And now, at last, they were all set.

Buddy Knox sang the vocals on the well-rehearsed "Party Doll" with its gaggle of background vocalists, volunteer sock cymbal player, newly recruited slap bass player, and David Alldred, the true professional, comfortably playing fifties rock and roll/Rockabilly on a slightly oversized cotton-filled cardboard box. Jimmy Bowen waited for his turn to sing the lead vocal on "I'm Stickin' with You," hoping for the same excitement and energy that Buddy displayed on "Party Doll"—and I must say, more than fifty years later, Buddy's performance is truly memorable and a major reason that this magical recording has lived a charmed life and royally entertained millions of happy people over the decades.

One folklore rumor has it that the original recording session in April 1956 was really planned for Jimmy Bowen, with Buddy Knox and the Rhythm Orchids backing Bowen on all songs. The rumor claims that Bowen put up all of the money for the session—all sixty bucks of it—and also furnished the car that carried the group to Clovis for the midnight-to-dawn session.

WHATEVER THE REAL STORY, THE RESULTS ARE CLEAR: "PARTY DOLL" AND BUDDY KNOX ARE THE HISTORIC STARS OF THIS AMAZING RECORDING.

The sixty-dollar recording session had to be the most exciting and luckiest recording session ever, for it created two multimillion-selling single recordings for Buddy Knox and Jimmy Bowen and gave Buddy Knox and the Rhythm Orchids an opportunity to meet new friends for life, who sang and played on their mammoth recordings. It also gave their new friends and family members something very historic to tell their grandchildren about: How they just happened to be hanging out one night at a small recording studio in Clovis, New Mexico, when suddenly they were plunged into American music history by volunteering to perform on two of the biggest foundational rock and roll recordings ever.

Life presents us with an amazing maze of unwitting surprises. Just ask Buddy Knox and the rest of the other folks who were just hanging around at a midnight-to-dawn recording session in April 1956 at Norman Petty's home studio. Like my longtime friend and production partner Tommy Overstreet once said to Donnie Lanier, "Whatever the real story, 'I'm Stickin' with You!'"

The Rhythm Orchids decided to set up its own record label with the name Triple D Records, named for the local pop radio station, KDDD Radio, in Dumas, Texas. Finally, Buddy Knox and the Rhythm Orchids were in the record business for real. When an Amarillo, Texas, disc jockey named Dean Kelly played "Party Doll" and "I'm Stickin' with You" on the radio, it quickly became a local hit—but it was destined for bigger things than that.

Donnie Lanier's sister, Teddy Lanier, was a fashion model for shoes at Andrew Geller and Company in New York City. Teddy took a couple of the "Party Doll" records to music publisher Phil Kahl, who passed them along to Morris Levy, the co-owner of Roulette Records. Levy loved the recordings but felt confused by the two vocalists on the one record. So he split up the record with Buddy Knox and the Rhythm Orchids on "Party Doll" and Jimmy Bowen and the Rhythm Orchids on "I'm Stickin' with You," and then separately released the two records nationally.

Phil Kahl became the personal manager of both Buddy Knox and Jimmy Bowen, and Roulette Records assisted in national promotion of the records by securing *The Ed Sullivan Show*, plus other television and national personal appearances for the boys.

In short order, Buddy Knox's "Party Doll" zoomed up the national *Billboard* charts to number one, sold over one million records and stayed on the national charts for twenty-three weeks. Jimmy Bowen's "I'm Stickin' with You" followed right behind with a bit less steam and peaked at number fourteen on the national *Billboard* charts; it also sold one million records.

Together, these recordings represent the first two million-selling single Rockabilly/fifties rock and roll records to come out of West Texas and the legendary Norman Petty studio. Their amazing and unexpected success showed a bunch of other West Texas hopefuls that it really *was* possible.

All of us had sixty dollars we wanted to spend!

"It was all total luck and fate," says Michael Knox, Buddy's son. "You know the typical star story: The ones who hit it huge, hit it by accident."

There might have been better, more equipped studios around the country than Sun Recording Studio and the Norman Petty Recording Studio, but those places didn't have Buddy Knox or Elvis Presley, Buddy Holly, Carl Perkins, or Johnny Cash walking through the doors. That's what made a studio more than a studio: The fact that guys like these could walk in, each with their unique styles and most with their own original songs—and these studios just let them do their thing.

The success of Buddy Knox's "Party Doll" session drew Buddy Holly to the Norman Petty studio a few months later. "Party Doll" is a magnet. It's a living Rockabilly/fifties rock and roll classic, still one of the most played records in broadcast history. It has now sold over fifteen million copies worldwide.

It was Buddy Knox who really motivated the local Rockabilly movement in West Texas. After Elvis Presley's first January 1955 performances on those three nights in West Texas, the area had become a proving ground for Rockabilly—and Buddy Knox became its charter test pilot. He also was one of the first in the history of rock and roll to write and sing his own number one hit. Buddy Knox was the first West Texan to get a gold record—before Buddy Holly and The Crickets and before Roy Orbison. In all, Buddy Knox ended up with four gold platters on his wall.

YOU CAN'T HARDLY LISTEN TO A BUDDY KNOX SONG
AND NOT SMILE. IT'S JUST THAT KIND OF MUSIC.

– CHARLIE DANIELS, SINGER, SONGWRITER, MUSICIAN, AND PERFORMER

SO CALL HIM THE HAPPY MAN FROM HAPPY, TEXAS. IN FACT, BUDDY ALWAYS SEEMED HAPPY. HE WAS A GOOD FRIEND, GENEROUS AND TRUSTWORTHY. HE WOULD BOLSTER YOU UP WHEN YOU FELT DOWN. HE ALSO WOULD GIVE YOU VERY SOUND ADVICE AND THEN HELP YOU LIVE IT.

Buddy Knox wasn't always happy with everything, of course. Eventually he left Roulette Records, as he said, because "They wouldn't let us—the Rhythm Orchids—participate in the production of our records as we had done with our first million sellers with Norman Petty. They were taking us down the wrong direction. They were making us record smooth, puffy-type rock and roll. We only wanted to record what made us successful—that good ol' Tex-Mex Rockabilly/rock and roll. They just didn't understand Rockabilly, which is what made us what we are. You would think they would have seen what made us and them successful. Also, Roulette Records had trouble with its accounting system; we sold over four million records with them, and they wouldn't pay us our record royalties—so we just left."

Buddy Knox followed "Party Doll" with "Rock Your Little Baby to Sleep" and "Hula Love." Each single sold over one million records and mastered the top of the national *Billboard* charts. Buddy also appeared on Ed Sullivan's television show and in several movies. By the end of his very successful career, he had earned eight additional top one hundred hits.

When "Party Doll" became a hit, Buddy Knox started touring eleven months of the year throughout the United States, Canada, and the UK. Buddy loved England and England loved Buddy. His son Michael said of him, "He really wanted to tour; that was his life, and that's all he knew. After 'Party Doll' hit number one, he made a commitment to perform for the rest of his life."

Buddy Knox looked into our *Tribute to the Rockabilly Legends* television cameras and said, "If I could do this till I was ninety years old, I would do it. And I may do it yet."

Buddy and I cowrote several songs that he recorded, including "She's Gone" and "Three Way Love Affair." "She's Gone" became a hit for Buddy in England and other countries. Buddy and I also toured together throughout the United States and Canada. I also enjoyed performing at Buddy's Purple Steer nightclub in Vancouver, British Columbia, Canada. It was a classy venue, and the fans were wonderful—just like Buddy himself, happy and wonderful.

Buddy Knox traced his musical education back to some familiar roots. "I grew up on a farm, and when we finished our chores at night, we had nothin' to do," he said. "We didn't have television . . . we had a big old radio that ran off a small generator. We only played the radio when my parents wanted to hear a specific show. They'd gather around that radio like people now gather around the TV, and they'd listen to country music programs like the Grand Ole' Opry from Nashville, or The Louisiana Hayride from Shreveport, Louisiana. When the program was over, they'd shut the radio down and turn the wind charger and the generator off."

If it sounds like Buddy had fun with his music, it's because he really did. Knox never tired of his job. He never grew weary of getting out in front of a crowd and trying to make them happy. And since Rockabilly influenced so much that came later, Buddy wanted people to understand its heritage. He wanted Rockabilly to get the credit it's due.

Buddy Knox's career and self-written recordings are critical to the fifties rock and roll/Rockabilly anthology. That's one of the main reasons I scheduled a trip to Buddy's home in Bremerton, Washington, for mid-February 1999, to document more of his personal contributions to Rockabilly from his unique perspective. I also was long overdue in visiting my long-time friend.

BUDDY
KNOX

Sadly, just before our scheduled meeting, I received a telephone call that Buddy had lost his fight with cancer, just nine days after doctors diagnosed him with the disease. I felt angry that I hadn't gone earlier to visit and very lonely because I knew I would never again have one of our great conversations, share a great laugh, or be able to write another song with my precious friend and collaborator.

Buddy Knox was truly a Rockabilly Legend. He deserves all of the accolades we can give him. This fifties rock and roll pioneer deserves to be honored with induction into the Rock and Roll Hall of Fame and Museum—and perhaps that overdue accolade will soon be bestowed on him.

I fondly remember and applaud all the great times, some of the low times, and most of all, Buddy Wayne Knox's unmatchable contributions to the world of fifties rock and roll that we called Rockabilly.

Buddy Wayne Knox: July 20, 1933 — February 14, 1999

LET'S THINK ABOUT LIVING, LET'S THINK ABOUT LIFE

It may appear to have nothing to do with a red Cadillac or a baseball contract, but then it may have everything to do with each of them. I'd like to tell you a little story about a songwriter who saved the career of one of my best friends.

Boudleaux (pronounced Bood-lo) Bryant literally saved the career of a young Rockabilly pal of mine by writing a little story on a stray piece of paper late one night. The story has a feeling of desperation that recalls many current songs of our own day. And then the writer makes a very powerful statement, which each of us perhaps should attempt to live by for the rest of our lives. The story goes like this:

In every other song that I've heard lately, some fellow gets shot. And his baby and his best friend both die with him, as likely as not. In half of the other songs, some cat's crying or ready to die. We've lost most of our happy people, and I'm wondering why.

Then comes the offer of reason:

Let's think about living. Let's think about loving. Let's think about the whoopin' and hoppin' and boppin' and the lovie, lovie dovin.' Let's forget about the whinin' and the cryin' and the shootin' and the dyin' and the fellow with the switchblade knife. Let's think about living—let's think about life!

Actually, that's not a bad idea for a hit song. Come to think of it, that's *exactly* what Don and Phil Everly thought the night they visited my pal Bob Luman while he was performing at the Golden Nugget Casino in downtown Las Vegas back in 1959.

Now, Bob had suffered some major disappointments in his singing career to that point and had his eye well trained on the ball—professional baseball, that is. Luman had just been offered a second chance to play with the Pittsburgh Pirates. He'd dumped his first Pirates contract in '56 because he felt eaten up with the Elvis virus; so he ran off, kicking and scratching, for a Rockabilly singing contract with The Louisiana Hayride in Shreveport, Louisiana.

Well, before I get too far, perhaps it would be better if I start this story at the beginning and then come back to this "Think About Living" thing.

"THIS CAT CAME OUT IN RED PANTS AND A GREEN COAT AND A PINK SHIRT AND SOCKS," BOB RECALLED YEARS LATER ABOUT HIS ELVIS ENCOUNTER,
"AND HE HAD THIS SNEER ON HIS FACE AND HE STOOD BEHIND THE MIC FOR FIVE MINUTES, I'LL BET, BEFORE HE MADE A MOVE. THEN HE HIT THE
GUITAR A LICK, AND HE BROKE TWO STRINGS. I'D BEEN PLAYING THAT GUITAR FOR TEN YEARS, AND I HADN'T BROKEN A TOTAL OF TWO STRINGS.
SO THERE HE WAS, WITH THESE TWO STRINGS JUST DANGLING, AND HE HADN'T DONE ANYTHING EXCEPT BREAK THESE STRINGS, YET ALL THESE
HIGH SCHOOL GIRLS WERE SCREAMING AND FAINTING AND RUNNING UP TO THE STAGE. AND THEN HE STARTED TO MOVE HIS HIPS REAL SLOW LIKE
HE HAD A THING FOR HIS GUITAR. HE MADE CHILLS RUN UP YOUR BACK, MAN, LIKE WHEN YOUR HAIR STARTS GRABBING AT YOUR COLLAR.
FOR THE NEXT NINE DAYS HE PLAYED ONE-NIGHTERS AROUND KILGORE, AND AFTER SCHOOL EVERY DAY ME AND MY GIRL WOULD GET IN THE CAR
AND GO WHEREVER HE WAS PLAYING THAT NIGHT. THAT'S THE LAST TIME I TRIED TO SING LIKE WEBB PIERCE OR LEFTY FRIZZELL.
I THREW MY COUNTRY SONGBOOK AWAY."

During the summer of 1955, Bob Luman was hitting baseballs into the bleachers in his hometown of Kilgore, Texas. He was just about to graduate from high school and was planning a career move to professional baseball in Pittsburgh, Pennsylvania.

Elvis Presley, Scotty Moore, and Bill Black had just played those famous dates in West Texas in January 1955, and now Elvis was rockin' the real estate of *East* Texas like a two-pronged tornado. When Bob Luman experienced the mighty madness of Elvis, he instantly gave up his promising baseball career and resigned himself to never wearing the uniform of the Pirates, the pro team that had recruited him out of high school.

With his new Rockabilly song list and a fire burning in his gut, Bob Luman answered a call for an amateur singing contest in Tyler, Texas, headlined by Johnny Cash, Johnny Horton, and George Jones (who appeared at the event for the handsome fee of fifty dollars). Contestants were to come by at 1 p.m. and audition before Tillman Franks. Tillman and Johnny Horton were flat broke at the time, and the only thing that earned them food and gasoline to get to their better dates on the weekends was doing these small town amateur shows. The winner of the amateur singing contest was offered a performance slot on the Saturday night Louisiana Hayride show.

Bob Luman arrived late for the auditions. Tillman had shut them down at 3 p.m. sharp. Bob strolled in, walked up to Tillman, and said, "I want to be on your amateur show."

"What's your name?" Tillman asked.

"Bob Luman."

"Well, you're too late now. We closed the auditions."

"Well, I can sing," Bob insisted. "I want to be on your show and win a contest."

"Sing me a song," Tillman said.

"I'll do a country song," Bob answered.

"Who do you sound like?" Tillman asked.

"Who do you want me to sound like?" Luman quipped.

"Sing one of Webb Pierce's songs." So Bob sang one of Webb's songs—and Tillman swore he sang it better than Webb did himself.

"Well, sing me an Elvis song."

And the same thing happened.

"Boy, you're good," Tillman declared. "You're on the show tonight."

Before the night was out, Bob had won the prize money and the Hayride slot—and tore the house down doing it. As a matter of fact, not only did he win, but Johnny Horton and Johnny Cash were standing backstage, cheering for him. They had heard Bob in the audition, and they told Tillman that if the boy didn't win, they were going to bring him down to The Louisiana Hayride anyway and put him on all their shows. Horace Logan, the general manager of the Hayride, following Tillman's recommendation, signed Bob to a contract to be a regular performer.

I met Bob Luman when I first went to perform on the Hayride. Through the years we worked many shows together. Our professional singing careers began at almost the same time. Both of us had that same "Elvis" experience, which drove us the same way it did Buddy Holly, Roy Orbison, Gene Vincent, and Johnny Horton. Elvis had opened the door for us, given us that freedom to do what we craved. We could sing what we loved, what we felt, and have our musicians play the gritty, gutsy Rockabilly backing we needed to push along the performance. It was an exciting time to be a pioneer of this new, exciting music.

Bob pieced together a little band that included the fifteen-year-old Shreveport, Louisiana, guitarist James Burton. In years to come this phenomenal musician would find his way to induction into the Rock and Roll Hall of Fame and Museum by way of working with Rick Nelson, Elvis, Roy Orbison, and EmmyLou Harris, among others.

In 1957, Bob went to Dallas, Texas, to record a classic little song titled "A Red Cadillac and a Black Moustache," accompanied by James Burton. With this record in hand he signed a contract with Lou Chud's Imperial Record label in Los Angeles, California, and the Bob Luman rocket had left the launching pad.

Unfortunately for Bob, Lou had also signed the young television star Rick Nelson to Imperial Records, and when Chud brought Bob and his band out to California for some sessions, Rick heard the band rehearsing and immediately hired James Burton and another two musicians away from Luman.

After losing his band—coupled with the fact that his records were not making it onto the national charts—Bob struggled to find his place in the music world. By 1959, Bob was just about to give up on his musical career—and now we're full circle from our beginning.

Bob started spending most of his time on the baseball diamond, practicing his favorite sport in an attempt to get another try at the majors. At night he was booked to perform at the Showboat Casino, a Las Vegas showcase for up-and-coming performers. One night Don and Phil Everly—The Everly Brothers—came by to catch his show. At the time, The Everly Brothers were the hottest fifties rock and roll/Rockabilly act in the world. "Bye Bye, Love," "Wake Up, Little Susie," and "All I Have to Do Is Dream" had each sold over one million records—and each of these songs had been written by the same man who made that philosophical statement I quoted earlier about "Let's Think About Living." His name is Boudleaux Bryant, and at that time he and his wife Felice just happened to be the hottest songwriters in America.

The Everly Brothers loved Bob Luman's Elvis-like performance and approached Bob to record a song written by their friend Boudleaux Bryant. Don and Phil insisted, "Bob, this song is perfect for you."

Luman felt flattered and grateful, but was just about to bottom out emotionally with disappointment over his faltering musical career. "No," Bob replied, "I think I'm going to quit this singing business and go back to baseball."

"You need to listen to this song first," the brothers insisted. "We just heard you sing, and we think this song is made for you."

Well, Bob *did* listen to the song and he did love it. He recorded it for Warner Brothers records and "Let's Think About Living" became a million-seller—a top-ten hit on both the national *BillBoard* country and pop charts.

Thanks to the insistence and good ears of The Everly Brothers, Bob Luman's career finally revved into high gear, with national television appearances on *The Ed Sullivan Show* and *The Dick Clark Show*. He even starred in a movie titled *Carnival Rock*. Bob's follow-up recording, "The Great Snowman," also became a top-ten hit on both the country and pop charts.

Bob moved to Nashville and began recording country music records with great success. By 1965 he was invited to become a member of the Grand Ole' Opry's family of entertainers. Bob Luman had truly arrived. His performances remained as energetic and rocking as in those early days of Rockabilly, and he stole the show everywhere he played.

I left the Crickets in the summer of 1965 for a television contract with ABC Television Network's *Shindig* music show, produced by England's great Jack Good, and for a solo recording and performing career. By 1967, I moved to Nashville to fulfill a contract to host a one-hour weekly television variety show called *Music City U.S.A.* This allowed me to have a reunion with my good pal Bob Luman, who also had signed on as a weekly performer. The show also featured that funnyman and singer-songwriter, Ray Stevens, as well as a bright young singer from Canada named Debbie Lori Kaye. We had a powerful lot of fun weaving in and out of excellent guest artists like Dolly Parton, the Jordanaires, and Jerry Reed, among others.

BOB LUMAN

WITH COUNTRY MUSIC CLASSIC HITS SUCH AS "WHEN YOU SAY YOU LOVE ME," "LONELY WOMEN MAKE GOOD LOVERS," AND "NEITHER ONE OF US (WANTS TO BE THE FIRST TO SAY GOODBYE)," BOB LUMAN HEADLINED GRAND OLE' OPRY TOURS THROUGHOUT THE UNITED STATES AND CANADA AND WAS THE FIRST COUNTRY STAR TO PERFORM IN PUERTO RICO. WITH THIS SUCCESS, BOB'S EARLY ROCKABILLY RECORDINGS RESURFACED AS INTERNATIONAL ROCKABILLY COLLECTABLES.

In 1978, our mutual friend and former Louisiana Hayride partner Johnny Cash produced the record "Alive and Well" with his longtime pal Bob Luman. Sadly, shortly afterward, despite the meaningful title of the new recording, Bob Luman collapsed after a performance on the Grand Ole' Opry and died at the young age of forty-one.

Given notice of Bob's death, I felt overcome with the thought, *Let's forget about the whinin' and the cryin', the shootin' and the dyin', and the fellow with the switchblade knife. Let's think about living. Let's think about life.*

I had to focus on Bob Luman's life.

If Bob Luman had lived, he would have continued to be one of the top country and pop music stars of our time.

Many people probably remember Bob as a country performer, but that's not the way he wanted to be known. Rockabilly artist Ronnie Weiser once reported, "When I saw Bob Luman in the 1970s, in the middle of the hippie onslaught and the sugary sissy 'Nashville Sound'—and when very few Americans even knew what the word 'Rockabilly' meant—I asked him, 'Bob, do you consider yourself a country singer or a Rockabilly singer?' Bob Luman roared back without any hesitation whatsoever: 'I'm ROCKABILLY!!'"

And that's how I remember him, too.

Bobby Glynn Luman: April 15, 1937 — December 27, 1978

WHEN I TALK ABOUT A ROCKABILLY LEGEND WHO GREW UP ON A COTTON FARM IN ARKANSAS, WHO DO YOU THINK ABOUT? THE MAN I'M THINKING OF WAS FIRST BATHED IN SOUTHERN GOSPEL MUSIC PLAYED BY HIS MOTHER ON THE SMALL RURAL CHURCH PIANO. SOUND FAMILIAR?

HE GOT HIS FIRST PIANO FIX FROM AN ELDERLY BLACK FIELDWORKER/PIANO BLUESMAN WHO CHOPPED AND PICKED COTTON. ON SATURDAY NIGHTS, HE LISTENED TO THE GRAND OLE' OPRY ON THE FAMILY RADIO, HUNGERING FOR INSPIRATION FROM HANK WILLIAMS, ROY ACUFF, JIMMIE RODGERS, AND BILL MONROE. THEN, AS SOON AS HE COULD, THE HUNGER IN HIS SOUL FOR A MUSIC CAREER DRAGGED HIM TO THE ROAD FOR TWENTY DOLLARS PER NIGHT ONE-NIGHT STANDS, WHERE HE WAS HEAVILY INFLUENCED BY THE DOWN-HOME BLUES OF B. B. KING, BOBBY "BLUE" BLAND, AND A YOUNG RAY CHARLES.

OH, THOSE L

ONELY WEEKENDS

This man played piano and sang for tips in juke joints throughout Tennessee, Louisiana, Mississippi, and Arkansas and quickly learned how to dodge flying bottles and duck drunks as they tumbled off the dance floor, fighting. In the early fifties this was known as the "chitlin' circuit."

So who comes to your mind? Is it Johnny Cash? Carl Perkins? Jerry Lee Lewis? Elvis? Well, actually, it's the legendary "Silver Fox," the shy, gentle bluesman of Sun Records—Charlie Rich.

CHARLIE RICH WAS AT THE SAME TIME ONE OF THE MOST SUCCESSFUL AND ONE OF THE MOST ERRATIC COUNTRY MUSIC SINGING STARS THE MUSIC INDUSTRY HAD EVER PRODUCED. RICH HAD ALL THE TALENT IN THE WORLD: POWERFUL VOICE, CLASSIC SONGWRITING ABILITY, AND A NATURAL PIANO STYLE.

Charlie, to some degree, loved most genres of music: gospel, country, pop, delta blues, and classical; but mostly Charlie loved the quiet complexity of *jazzie blues*. And he played and sang that jazz-blues blend very well at a very young age, urged on by his high school music teacher, Andrew Clements, who was originally a jazz and blues musician from Chicago's Blue Note set.

Add to all of this Charlie's testimony that Jerry Lee Lewis also heavily influenced him, and one begins to realize that we are not dealing with some run-of-the-mill Rockabilly artist, but with a complicated giant of prodigious musical ability who was waiting to explode into superstardom.

In the beginning, Charlie Rich found the "commercialized" music of fifties rock and roll/Rockabilly to be a bit disorganized and too confusing for his tastes; but at the same time, he loved the challenge of the rhythms, and he *really* loved the new stars of this genre, men he met at Sun Records: Elvis Presley, Carl Perkins, Johnny Cash, Roy Orbison, and, of course, "The Killer," Jerry Lee Lewis.

"At first," Charlie admitted, "I didn't dig country. As a matter of fact, we put it down because we wanted to be jazz pickers. I had to make a drastic change at Sun Records, and I didn't really appreciate this country and Rockabilly music until I went there. It was Jerry Lee Lewis who really opened my eyes to it."

Charlie Rich also explained his evolution to the mega-million-selling country-pop crossover hits "Behind Closed Doors" and "The Most Beautiful Girl."

"It was Ray Charles who later meshed all these things together for me—jazz, blues, gospel, fifties rock and roll/Rockabilly, and country. When Ray came out with those country soul albums, I really felt *that* in a big way. He had a big band, vocal group background singers, his piano—you know, the whole thing. It was exciting to me, and that's exactly the kind of recording I wanted to do."

It took a while for all the elements of Charlie's complex background to come together. But when they finally did, *ka-blam*! Charlie himself spoke of the many musical influences in his life like this: "My daddy was a cotton farmer and a singer. I started singing real young when my folks were singing gospel music. My mother played those great old gospel songs on the piano, and my dad sang in a Southern gospel quartet. I cherished the sounds of the black field hands singing those old spirituals. It chilled me and from that very early age, I felt the rhythm deep inside me. I felt the tug of the gospel. I dreamed in colors of music, and my colors were mostly blues."

In high school, Charlie started singing more seriously, "to some degree." Mr. Clements, his music teacher, was an excellent choir director and a talented piano teacher. He drew Charlie closer toward the center of great jazz. "I've often said that I was born with gospel, bathed in the blues, and schooled in jazz," Charlie said. "I love them all."

Charlie Rich began his career while in the U.S. Air Force in the early fifties. While stationed at Enid Air Force Base in Oklahoma, Charlie formed a group called the Velvatones, which played jazz and blues and featured his fiancée, Margaret Ann, on lead vocals.

Soon Margaret Ann became Charlie's wife, as well as his biggest supporter. She did everything in her power to advance her husband's career. When Charlie met Bill Justice, Margaret Ann asked Bill to listen to some of Charlie's tapes and try to get him an audition. Bill and Sam Phillips liked what they heard and hired Charlie as a session player for Roy Orbison, Johnny Cash, and Jerry Lee Lewis. Margaret Ann was a great songwriter in her own right, and she and Charlie made an excellent songwriting team. Early in their association with Sun, Charlie and Margaret Ann wrote "Break Up" for Jerry Lee Lewis, "The Ways of a Woman in Love" for Johnny Cash, and "I'm Coming Home" for Elvis Presley.

So as early as 1956, Charlie was playing piano on various Sun sessions, but Sam wouldn't let him record anything that might compete with Elvis. Still, Sam loved Charlie's performances, his unique, rich vocal performance, his deep soul, and his obvious talent. Charlie did amazing things, especially as an inexperienced musician and singer. He'd sit at the piano, look up at the mic and sing a number a single time, and that was it. And if he did sing it again, it was no better than his first attempt. Even on the demo sessions, he'd nail them on the first take.

It was the end of the decade, however, before Charlie Rich got the opportunity to show just how much he had to offer. "Lonely Weekends" is classic Charlie Rich and an historic Rockabilly contribution for the waning years of Sun. Yet it would be yet another decade before the world would *really* know the true creative depth of this great artist.

Margaret and I wrote it for Jerry Lee Lewis, or at least we thought we had. We really wanted him to record it. He was hotter than a firecracker about then. We didn't have a demo on it, other than a little homemade tape, which wasn't too good. So we went into Sun, and at one of those loose, somewhat dis-organized demonstration recording session situations—typical for Sun in those days—we cut the demo. Sam Phillips liked it. He liked the sound of it really well and he said, "Why don't you just cut it yourself, Charlie?" I didn't know if this was a put-down or what. I thought Sam didn't think it was good enough for Jerry Lee Lewis. But, come to find out, Sam actually liked it so much he wanted me to record it, and that's what we did. Jack Clement, Johnny Cash and Jerry Lee's record producer, and Bill Justice helped us and it became my first hit.

Charlie paused for a moment and then pensively said, "Sam had a great ear and also had a great sense for being able to get the best out of people—especially musicians or performing people. That had a lot to do with the success of Sun Records."

At that point in the interview, Charlie spread his hands over the keys and began to sing, *"Well, I make it all right from Monday morning 'til Friday night, But OOOOOHHHH those lonely weekends…"* I joined in singing harmony with him, and we did about three-quarters of the song, live, with just that old studio piano. What a thrill!

After he finished, I said, "Okay, let's move forward. You've got a brand-new record just coming out. Tell me about it." Rather than saying anything, Charlie placed his big hands on the piano keys and played those three famous chords—*bling, bling, bling*—and as smooth as butter, rolled out the rest of that amazing Hargus "Pig" Robbins piano intro. Then Charlie raised his head to the mic and began singing a lyric with more soul than I'd ever experienced that live and up close:

My baby makes me proud. Lord, don't she make me proud, She never makes a scene by hangin' all over me in crowd, Well, People like to talk. Lord, how they love to talk, But when they turn out the lights, I know she'll be leavin' with me….. And, When you get behind closed doors….

It was beyond wonderful. When you hear that little piano introduction, you just have to turn it up all the way. The unique, personal, live performance of this great classic from Charlie Rich on our radio show cast a moment in time I'll never forget. I was blessed to be at that place at that moment, and I am honored to count Charlie Rich as a close friend.

Charlie's premature death in 1995 at age sixty-three touched me deeply. Touring the country and the world for so many years and living out of hotel rooms for weeks at a time, I have always harbored a fear of someday dying alone in one of those rooms. Red Foley passed away this way, alone in a motel room while on tour—and I never could deal properly with the incident.

When the news came that Charlie Rich had also died in his sleep—from a blood clot in his lung, in a hotel room while traveling to Florida for a performance—I couldn't shake the deep, anxious feelings that swept over me. It seems all we live is "one-night stands, performing on that stage, and lonely hotel rooms." And as I fought tears of grief, I kept asking myself the same question I have asked since the early sixties: "Where do I go when the show closes?"

During his too few years on earth, Charlie Rich gave hundreds of fantastic performances that wowed audiences all over the world. He helped Rockabilly gain a foothold in the music world, and along with the other Legends, he'll never be forgotten.

As the man who first recorded Charlie Rich and literally launched his career, Sam Phillips summed up his personal feelings about Charlie Rich: "I don't think I ever recorded anyone who was a better singer, writer, and player than Charlie Rich. It's all so easy—so effortless, the way he moved from rock to country to blues to jazz. Charlie Rich took what was before him and did an exceptional job with it!"

Margaret Ann had her own take on the genius that was her husband. With tongue planted firmly in cheek, Charlie's loving wife once said, "As a cotton farmer, Charlie was a pretty good piano player." Yes, indeed. And then some.

Charlie Rich: December 14, 1934 — July 25, 1995

GOLDEN

GLOVES, SILVER VOICES

Johnny and Dorsey Burnette, assisted by their friend/guitarist Paul Burlison, jumped ahead of history in 1953 by rocking up the traditional country songs of the day and performing forbidden up-tempo, segregated black songs in the joints around Memphis, Tennessee. In fact, they were the first musical pioneers who helped to found Rockabilly music—a year *before* Elvis Presley's Big Bang "accident" of 1954.

This trio of change-hungry musicians had been baptized into the depths of the delta blues by the one and only gut-wrenching Beale Street Memphis bluesman, Howlin' Wolf himself. No one could possibly come within six counties of the Howlin' Wolf's performances and walk away unaffected. Like another legendary guitar bluesman, Robert Johnson, the Wolf's heavy, dark renditions haunted your very soul and had a way of burrowing deep inside you and growing.

When Paul Burlison got out of the navy, he often visited West Memphis, where Howlin' Wolf did a radio show. Paul adapted a lot of the Wolf's pushy, aggressive guitar style, and together with the Burnette brothers, the trio invented the essentials of Rockabilly: the slapping bass, the aggressive guitar, the rhythm guitar, no drums. They formed a group called The Rock and Roll Trio, then Johnny Burnette and the Rock and Roll Trio, and finally The Johnny Burnette Trio.

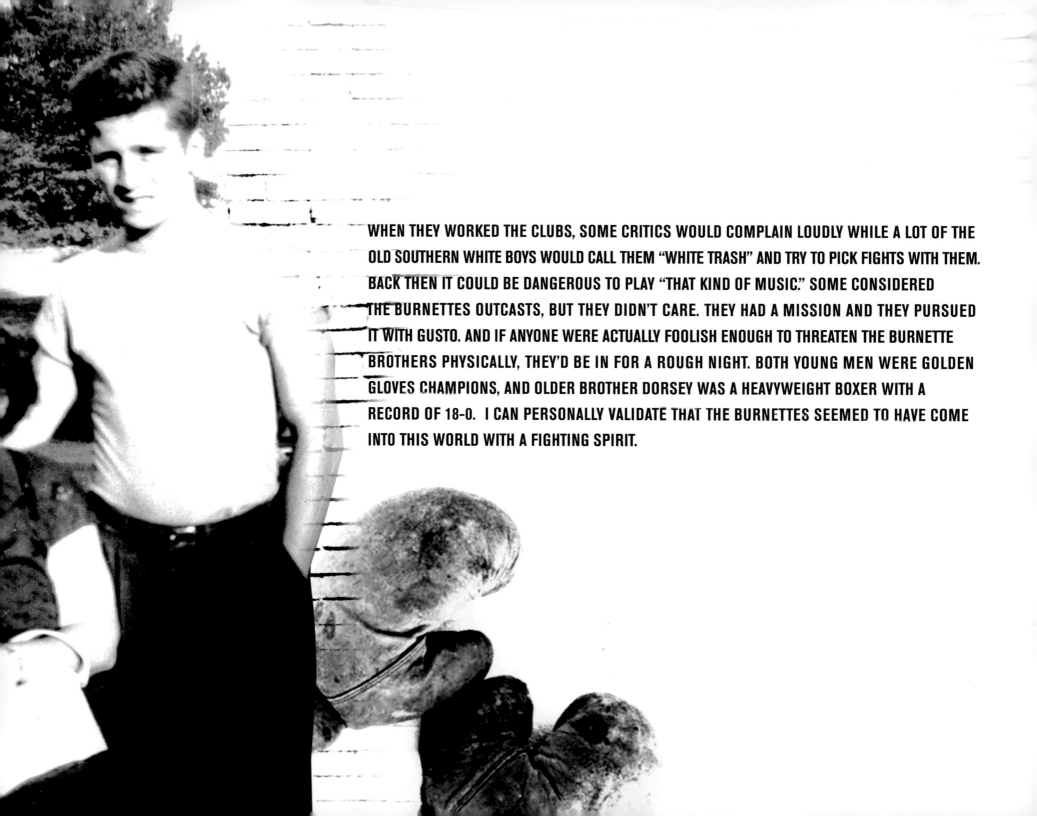

WHEN THEY WORKED THE CLUBS, SOME CRITICS WOULD COMPLAIN LOUDLY WHILE A LOT OF THE OLD SOUTHERN WHITE BOYS WOULD CALL THEM "WHITE TRASH" AND TRY TO PICK FIGHTS WITH THEM. BACK THEN IT COULD BE DANGEROUS TO PLAY "THAT KIND OF MUSIC." SOME CONSIDERED THE BURNETTES OUTCASTS, BUT THEY DIDN'T CARE. THEY HAD A MISSION AND THEY PURSUED IT WITH GUSTO. AND IF ANYONE WERE ACTUALLY FOOLISH ENOUGH TO THREATEN THE BURNETTE BROTHERS PHYSICALLY, THEY'D BE IN FOR A ROUGH NIGHT. BOTH YOUNG MEN WERE GOLDEN GLOVES CHAMPIONS, AND OLDER BROTHER DORSEY WAS A HEAVYWEIGHT BOXER WITH A RECORD OF 18-0. I CAN PERSONALLY VALIDATE THAT THE BURNETTES SEEMED TO HAVE COME INTO THIS WORLD WITH A FIGHTING SPIRIT.

From a very early age, Dorsey and Johnny were physical even with their musical instruments. Their father gave both of them Gene Autry guitars on the same day, when Dorsey was six and Johnny was four. The boys immediately gave the Singing Cowboy a licking—the brothers smashed the Gene Autry guitars into small pieces. Dad had to explain to his young sons that it really would be a lot more fun to play the instruments than to pound them to a pulp.

Elvis Presley—who along with the Burnettes and Paul Burlison lived at the Lauderdale Courts, a low-income federal housing project—used to call the brothers "the Daltons," after the infamous outlaw gang. They were a rough group, and everybody really was scared of them. Dorsey's son, Billy Burnette, remembers, "My mother said that when she met my dad, nobody would have anything to do with her, 'cause everyone was scared to death of them."

And these tough guys were playing what many back then called "the devil's music," adding to the Burnette-image folklore.

Rocky Burnette, Johnny's son, remembers, "They had that rock and roll spirit—they were both wild guys. They didn't like being told what to do. They liked doing things their own way. They liked making music their own way, and that's exactly what they did."

At the same time, as I can vouch from personal experience, if they considered you a friend, there was practically nothing they wouldn't do for you. You might fear them as enemies, but you loved them as friends.

Elvis often came around when the Burnette trio was rehearsing at Lauderdale Courts—and usually Dorsey would run him off. "Dad," Billy would later say, "you ran away the king of rock and roll!"

So why wouldn't they let Elvis sing with them? "He was just somebody bugging them," Billy answers. Elvis would pester them with a continual, "Teach me how to play the guitar," and they'd reply, "Get away from here, kid." Elvis also wanted to sing those pop crooner ballads, which they considered mushy. And there was no place in the world of the Burnette brothers for musical mush! Dorsey's future wife, Alberta, sometimes played basketball with Elvis, just to lure him away from the trio's practice sessions in the laundry room (where the concrete walls produced great echo). Elvis was just some kid who wanted to be part of the gang.

Some nights the Burnettes and Paul Burlison worked with a swing band. When the band took a break for intermission, the trio would play their hard, knock-down, raw music that didn't yet have a name. But that would soon change.

In two consecutive months in 1953, the Burnette brothers each had a son. Johnny named his son Rocky, while Dorsey named his newborn son Billy—both boys named after professional boxers. The proud fathers dedicated a week of their performances, and then a whole month, to their new babies. "This is a Rocky 'n' Billy song," they'd say, and they'd romp into "Tear It Up" or something else. Eventually they wrote a song called "Rocky 'n' Billy Boogie." Inevitably, someone in the crowd would forget the name of the song and call out, "Play that Rockabilly song."

To all of us who were there at the beginning, that's where Rockabilly really got its name. The Burnettes didn't record their song until after Elvis smashed his way into the history books, but they birthed the name for this new and vibrant world-changing music.

One of the Burnettes's songs, "Train Kept 'a Rollin'," became an early classic rock and roll trio song, considered by many to be the national anthem of Rockabilly. And you can hear the moving desperation in Johnny Burnette's voice in the song, "Lonesome Train on a Lonesome Track," which also features a slapping bass. They put their sweat and blood into all those songs. That's just the way they lived.

In early 1956, the trio of friends moved to New York City. One night while Dorsey went to a movie to watch a science fiction film, Johnny and Paul slipped into a television taping of *Ted Mack and the Original Amateur Hour*. Somehow these two inquisitive outlaws found out how they could audition their own act for the television show. After waiting for hours in line, they discovered they had six minutes to impress someone—and even after hearing that no new acts would get on the air for several months, they won a spot on the show the very next week. They won the competition for three weeks straight and earned a string of tour dates. That led to a recording contract with Coral Records, where they produced a string of Rockabilly classics: "Tear It Up," "Oh Baby Babe," "Honey Hush." They appeared on *The Steve Allen Show*, *American Bandstand*, and *The Perry Como Kraft Music Hall*. They also performed "Lonesome Train on a Lonesome Track" in the film *Rock Rock Rock*.

I first met Johnny and Dorsey Burnette shortly after I moved to California in early 1960 to become the lead singer for the Crickets. Everybody told me that these were the wildest guys I'd ever know. "They love to fight," I heard, "but they write *great* songs."

I already knew of many of those songs. They had written "It's Late" and "Believe What You Say" for Rick Nelson, both smash hits, among many others.

Their trio had broken up in 1957 and Johnny and Dorsey had moved to California and signed separate recording contracts with different companies. Johnny had two major hits on his own, "Dreamin'," on Liberty Records, the same record company the Crickets were recording on. "Dreamin'" reached number eleven on *Billboard*'s Hot 100, and "You're Sixteen," which reached number eight by the end of 1960. The latter song hit number three in England, where superstar-to-be Ringo Starr heard it and recorded his own smash version thirteen years later.

DORSEY WAS PROBABLY THE DEEPER WRITER OF THE TWO. HE WROTE AND RECORDED TWO NUMBER ONE HITS CALLED "TALL OAK TREE" AND THE CLASSIC "HEY LITTLE ONE," AND IN ALL WROTE MORE THAN 350 SONGS, COVERED BY ARTISTS SUCH AS RICK NELSON, JERRY LEE LEWIS, WAYLON JENNINGS, GLEN CAMPBELL, AND STEVIE WONDER (DORSEY HAD HEARD A YOUNG STEVIE PLAYING HIS HARMONICA ON A BEACH AND PROMPTLY TOOK THE BOY INTO A STUDIO FOR HIS FIRST RECORDING SESSION). BOB DYLAN CALLED DORSEY ONE OF THE GREATEST SONGWRITERS EVER. DORSEY SOON BECAME ONE OF MY CLOSEST FRIENDS. I HAD LOST MY MOTHER WHEN I WAS SIXTEEN, AND MY FATHER AND SIBLINGS STILL LIVED IN TEXAS, SO DORSEY AND ALBERTA BECAME MY FAMILY. AND IN 1964 I DISCOVERED JUST HOW MUCH I NEEDED THEM AND HOW CLOSE WE HAD GROWN.

In the early sixties we all were taking a lot of amphet-amines. Johnny Cash, Roger Miller, Hoyt Axton, Dorsey and Johnny, and I—we all abused them. We took them, we thought, because truck drivers took those things for long-haul driving, and we thought we had to do the same thing to drive our tours. I was the designated driver for the Crickets, and we drove to almost all our performances, whether throughout the U.S. or Canada. We bought a new Cadillac every year and pulled a small trailer behind the Caddy, filled with all of our gear. To keep up that kind of schedule, we took a lot of pills.

When I was just twenty-five, I had a massive coronary, a blowout from taking the pills. At the time we were working on a movie called *Girls on the Beach*, starring The Beach Boys, the Crickets, and Leslie Gore. We had one or two more days of shooting left at Malibu Beach, and I had lost so much weight (I was down to 114 pounds) that a friend kept telling me, "You're going to have a heart attack. You have all of the symptoms, you're not eating, you're not sleeping—and you're taking too many pills." I didn't drink alcohol, but I downed a lot of Coca-Cola.

Of course, I never thought, *I'm a drug addict*. You get started in it, establish a pattern, and it just takes over. One of the worst things is that the pills give you an exhilarating energy high; but when they wear off, they leave you with the worst depressive low imaginable. So obviously, you take more.

I went through three and a half years of that until I had a heart attack in May 1964. And true to their reputation, the Burnettes were the first people to show up to help. They put together a big benefit show for me because they didn't know how long I'd be out of work. In those days, no matter how much money you made, you spent a lot of it.

It took me the rest of that year to recover—and the Burnette brothers, along with Glen and Billie Campbell, stayed with me the whole time. Every day they looked for ways to support me, both emotionally and financially. "Keep your career going," they told me. Now, that's support! I can't imagine a family being any closer. These guys *were* my family.

Just three months after my brush with death, Dorsey suffered the biggest blow of his life. Some time after dark on August 14, 1964, at Clear Lake, California, a cabin cruiser rammed Johnny's tiny unlit fishing boat. The crash threw Johnny overboard and he drowned.

Dorsey never got over his loss. He responded by becoming a born-again Christian and moving even deeper into his writing, solo performing, and recording. And most important, we remained close friends and continued to work together right up until the night before he died.

The last time I saw him alive, we performed at Knott's Berry Farm. After we had a bite to eat, I left him about 2 a.m., when I had to go to work at KLAC radio in Los Angeles, the country music station where I worked as a DJ whenever I wasn't touring. At that time of morning, when you're on the air, you're there all by yourself. I went on the air at 6 a.m., and within the first half hour, I saw the red light of our studio hotline light up—a very rare occurrence. Only the program director, the station manager, and your personal family had that number. Well, Dorsey was still my family, and he and Alberta had the number.

I picked up the phone and heard Alberta's anxious voice on the other end as the most helpless feeling I ever had swept over me. "Dorsey is on the floor," she said. "I don't think he's breathing, and I need help."

"Oh, please," I answered, "call 911 immediately. I'll call someone as well. But I can't come there right now; I'm the only person here. Call me back as soon as someone gets there."

But in my heart, I knew he was dead—and he was. He had suffered a massive and fatal heart attack. He died on August 19, 1979, at forty-seven years of age. A tribute concert at the Forum in Inglewood featured Tanya Tucker, Glenn Campbell, Edward James Olmos, Kris Kristofferson, Duane Eddy, Gary Busey, Maureen McGovern, and others who also loved Dorsey and his incomparable musical contributions.

John Joseph Burnette: March 25, 1934 — August 14, 1964

Along with the Perkins brothers, Johnny and Dorsey Burnette paved the way for all of us. In fact, they had the courage to play what became Rockabilly before the rest of us. Or maybe it wasn't courage; maybe it was just that they had the innocence to do it before anyone else. They didn't know any better; they just did what they felt. And what they did was absolutely great.

So in one sense, Rockabilly was really born in 1953, in the Memphis area honky-tonks, through the often wild and creative efforts of Johnny, Dorsey, and Paul Burlison—The Johnny Burnette Trio. Their music was the absolute epitome of what is now and always has been Rockabilly. Had they recorded "Rockabilly Boogie" in 1953, before Elvis, the history of Rockabilly might have turned out completely different.

But even without that, their place as legendary Rockabilly performers remains secure. In their amazing body of work, they live on still, fighting as hard as ever for the music they so dearly loved.

Dorsey William Burnette, Jr.: December 28, 1932 — August 19, 1979

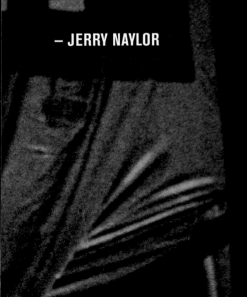

ELVIS OPENED THE DOOR FOR US. HE SAID, "NOW IT'S OKAY. YOU CAN GO THROUGH. YOU CAN GO OUT AND SING THE BLACK-ORIENTED RHYTHM AND BLUES SONGS AND DO 'EM YOUR WAY. YOU CAN ADD A LITTLE GOSPEL TO IT IF YOU WANT TO." UNTIL THEN WE'D ALL BEEN STYMIED. WE DIDN'T HAVE PERMISSION TO DO THAT UNTIL ELVIS CAME ALONG.

— JERRY NAYLOR

Elvis Aaron Presley: January 8, 1935 — August 16, 1977

Sitting left to right: Tillman Franks, Tommy Tomlinson, Gordon Terry, Jerry Naylor, Bob Luman, Luther Perkins
Standing left to right: Joe Treadway, Stu Cornell, Johnny Cash, Johnny Horton, Marshall Grant

EPILOGUE

As writer/musicologist Craig Morrison told us in the beginning, "Rockabilly is an emotionally intense and rhythmic blend [of music]." A new and unique *blend,* not unlike a good experience from your local Starbucks—but an extraordinary *custom* blend never imagined before these pioneer rockers created it.

John Carter Cash says of Rockabilly, "These are sounds which appear to be simple in musicianship and are great fun musically. Rockabilly opened the floodgates and put motion in music, which hadn't been known before. Our fathers recorded with grit, grime, and honesty—the beauty of this blend is evident when you hear every note of the music. Many try to play their music today, and most still don't understand its complicated simplicity—complicated because it came directly from their soul. These fifties rock/Rockabilly musicians were never trained musically; they were individually unique, but fed off each other. This music came through their instruments, from deep within themselves."

I thank God that I have been allowed to share the stories of my friends and our personal experiences of this great era with you. The energy, fun, and excitement of those early years remain as vivid today as when we first experienced them more than fifty years ago. The innocence and the energy we had, the need to just do what we felt; the beautiful rawness of the players, their youth, their vivaciousness, their vigor and hunger—you can *feel* the freshness of this legendary music deep in your heart.

I'm also very pleased we were able to restore and preserve this era of music for you and for generations to come. Let's enjoy it, play it, shout it, sing it, and celebrate it with all our hearts. This music makes you happy! It also makes you move—and fifty years from now, it will still make you move. It gets down into your soul.

As Uncle John told six-year-old Carl Perkins when he placed his firm, gentle hand over the skinny fingers of the youngster as they both clutched the guitar: "Carl, it ain't just in the guitar, it's in the fingers. What I mean by that is that it's in the soul. Get down close to it. You can feel it travel down the strangs, come through your head and down to your soul where you live. You can feel it. Let it *vi-ber-ate.*"

Rockabilly continues to "vi-ber-ate" through the classic works of these gifted originators, the Rockabilly Legends.

What Carl Perkins started with the first time he picked up his guitar, he ended with on his last day on earth. The man never changed—he always did the same thing, and he was always great. So it's only appropriate that the godfather of Rockabilly should have the last word:

I GUESS FEW PEOPLE GROW UP BETWEEN TWO COTTON ROWS WITHOUT ANY REASON TO BELIEVE, AS YOU PUT YOUR LITTLE COUNTRY EAR AGAINST A LITTLE BATTERY RADIO, AND DREAM OF WHAT THE STAGE OF THE GRAND OLE' OPRY LOOKS LIKE—AND YOU PUSH, THEN YOU PRAY, AND IN AMERICA, YOU CAN. SOMEDAY YOU CAN SING A SONG ABOUT SOME SHOES, YOUR BEST GIRLFRIEND, OR A PRISON, AND PEOPLE WILL CRY AND DANCE AND CHEER. DON'T TELL ME WE DON'T LIVE IN THE GREATEST COUNTRY IN THE WORLD! THIS IS AMERICA. THIS IS WHERE DREAMS CAN COME TRUE AND ROCKABILLY WILL LIVE FOREVER.

PHOTO CREDITS

COVER

Jerry Lee Lewis: Showtime Music Archive

Buddy Holly: Showtime Music Archive

Elvis Presley: Showtime Music Archive

Carl Perkins: Showtime Music Archive/Colin Escott

Johnny Cash: Showtime Music Archive

Roy Orbison: Showtime Music Archive/Pictorial Press/Tony Gale

Original painting by master artist George Hunt

BACK COVER

Lewis/Perkins/Presley/Cash: Showtime Music Archive

FRONT MATTER:

Pg. 1 Original painting by master artist George Hunt

Pg. 4 Arthur Crudup: Showtime Music Archive

Bill Monroe: Showtime Music Archive

Roy Acuff: Showtime Music Archive

Pg. 5 Hank Williams: Showtime Music Archive

Pg. 6-7 Gene Vincent and the Blue Caps: Showtime Music Archive

Pg. 8-9 Jerry and Pamela Naylor: Jerry Naylor Company LLC

INTRODUCTION:

Pg. 13 Jerry Naylor: Jerry Naylor Company LLC

Jerry Naylor: Jerry Naylor Company LLC

Pg. 14 Jerry Naylor: Jerry Naylor Company LLC

Jerry Naylor: Jerry Naylor Company LLC

Jerry Naylor: Jerry Naylor Company LLC

Pg. 18 Scotty Moore: Showtime Music Archive/Garet Gart

Pg. 19 Tillman Franks: Showtime Music Archive/Colin Escott

Pg. 20 Scotty Moore: Showtime Music Archive/Garet Gart

Pg. 21 Tillman Franks: Showtime Music Archive/Colin Escott

Pg. 22 Martin Luther King Jr.: Courtesy of the Library of Congress, LC-USZ62-122992

Pg. 23 Elvis Presley: Showtime Music Archive

Pg. 24 Presley/Moore/Black: Showtime Music Archive

CHAPTER 1

Pg. 27 Howlin Wolf: Showtime Music Elvis Presley: Showtime Music

Pg. 28-29 Elvis Presley: Showtime Music Archive/Robert C. Dye

Presley Ad: Showtime Music Archive

Pg. 30 Sam Phillips & Elvis Presley: Showtime Music Archive/ Colin Escott

Pg. 31 Sam Phillips & Carl Perkins: Showtime Music Archive/ Colin Escott

Sam Phillips & Johnny Cash: Showtime Music Archive/Colin Escott

Sam Phillips & Jerry Lee Lewis: Showtime Music Archive/Colin Escott

Pg. 32 Sam Phillips: Showtime Music Archive/Colin Escott

Pg. 34 Sun Studios: Showtime Music Archive

Pg. 35 Sun Studios Business Card: Showtime Music Archive

Pg. 36 Elvis, Scotty Moore and Bill Black: Showtime Music Archive

Pg. 39 Sun Record: Sun Entertainment , Inc.

Pg. 40-41 Bill Monroe: Showtime Music Archive

Pg. 42-43 Screaming Fans: Joseph Kent Jr./Louisianna Hayride Inc

Pg. 44 Elvis Presley: Showtime Music Archive/Colin Escott

Pg. 45 Elvis Presley: Showtime Music Archive

Pg. 46 Elvis Presley: Joseph Kent Jr./Louisianna Hayride Inc

Pg. 49 Elvis Presley: Buddy Wayne Knox Estate

Pg. 50 Tillman Franks: Showtime Music Archive/Colin Escott

Pg. 53 Elvis Presley/Louisiana Hayride: Joseph Kent Jr./ Louisianna Hayride Inc

Pg. 54-55 Tillman Franks/Johnny Horton: Tillman Franks Enterprises

CHAPTER 2

Pg. 59 Elvis Presley: Joseph Kent Jr./Louisianna Hayride Inc

Pg. 60-61 Elvis Presley: Showtime Music Archive/Colin Escott

Elvis Presley: Showtime Music Archive

Elvis Presley: Showtime Music Archive

Pg. 62-63 Buddy Holly: Showtime Music Archive/Pictorial Press

Pg. 64-65 Buddy Holly: Bill Griggs/Rockin' '50s Magazine

Pg. 66-67 Buddy Holly: Bill Griggs/Rockin' '50s Magazine

Pg. 69 Buddy Holly/Peggy Sue: Peggy Sue Gerron/
Rave On Productions

Pg. 72 Buddy Holly and the Crickets Albums: Showtime Music Archive

Pg. 73 Buddy Holly: Showtime Music Archive

Pg. 74-75 Buddy Holly and the Crickets: Bill Griggs/
Rockin' '50s Magazine

Pg. 76-77 Greenwich Village: andrew.cmu.edu

Pg. 79 Airplane Image: Bill Griggs/Rockin' '50s Magazine

Pg. 80-81 Buddy Holly: Bill Griggs/Rockin' '50s Magazine

Pg. 84 Buddy Holly and the Crickets: Showtime Music Archive/
Pictorial Press

Pg. 85 Buddy Holly: Showtime Music Archive

Pg. 86 Buddy Holly: Bill Griggs/Rockin' '50s Magazine

Pg. 88 Buddy Holly: Showtime Music Archive/Picotrial Press

Pg. 89 Fender Ad: Showtime Music Archive

Pg. 90-91 Buddy Holly: Showtime Music Archive

Pg. 92 Buddy Holly: Showtime Music Archive

Pg. 95 Roy Orbison: Showtime Music Archive/Pictorial Press/
Tony Gale

Pg. 96-97 Roy Orbison: Showtime Music Archive/Colin Escott

Pg. 99 Roy Orbison and the Teen Kings: Showtime Music Archive/
Colin Escott

Pg. 101 Roy Orbison: Showtime Music Archive/Colin Escott

Sam Phillips: Showtime Music Archive/Colin Escott

Pg. 102-103 Roy Orbison: Showtime Music Archive/Colin Escott

Sun Studios: Scott Petersen

Pg. 104 Roy Orbison: Showtime Music Archive/Colin Escott

Pg. 105 Roy Orbison Album: Showtime Music Archive

Pg. 106 Roy Orbison: Showtime Music Archive

Pg. 107 Roy Orbison Albums: Showtime Music Archive

Pg. 108 Roy Orbison: Showtime Music Archive/Pictorial Press/
Tony Gale

Pg. 109 Roy Orbison: Showtime Music Archive/Pictorial Press

Pg. 111 Roy Orbison: Showtime Music Archive/Colin Escott

Pg. 113 Roy Orbison: Showtime Music Archive

Pg. 114-115 Elvis Presely: Showtime Music Archive

CHAPTER 3

Pg. 117 White Church: N. Hesson/Nayco Ent.

Pg. 118-119 Guitar Player: Showtime Music Archive

Pg. 120-121 Carl Perkins: Showtime Music Archive/Colin Escott

Elvis Presley: Showtime Music Archive

Pg. 122-123 Carl Perkins: Showtime Music Archive

Pg. 124-125 Carl Perkins: Showtime Music Archive

Pg. 126 Carl Perkins Album: Showtime Music Archive

Pg. 128 Carl Perkins: Showtime Music Archive

Pg. 129 Carl Perkins: Showtime Music Archive/Colin Escott

Pg. 130-131 Carl Perkins Record: Showtime Music Archive

Pg. 132 Carl Perkins: Showtime Music Archive

Pg. 134 Carl Perkins and Johnny Cash: Showtime Music Archive/
Colin Escott

Pg. 136 Carl Perkins: Showtime Music Archive

Pg. 138 Carl Perkins: Showtime Music Archive

Pg. 140-141 Carl Perkins and Elvis Presley: Showtime Music Archive

Pg. 142 Carl Perkins with Guitar: Showtime Music Archive/
Colin Escott

Carl Perkins Recording: Showtime Music Archive/Colin Escott

Pg. 143 Carl Perkins: Showtime Music Archive/Bryan Smith/
Colin Escott

Pg. 144 Carl Perkins Preforming: Showtime Music Archive/
Bryan Smith/Colin Escott

Pg. 147 Carl Perkins: Showtime Music Archive/Colin Escott

PHOTO CREDITS CONT...

CHAPTER 4

Pg. 148 Johnny Cash: Showtime Music Archive

Pg. 149 Jerry Lee Lewis: Showtime Music Archive

Pg. 151 Johnny Cash: Showtime Music Archive

Pg. 152 Various Flyers: Showtime Music Archive

Pg. 154 Johnny Cash: Showtime Music Archive

Pg. 155 Johnny Cash: Showtime Music Archive/Colin Escott

Pg. 156-157 Luther Perkins, Johnny Cash, and Marshall Grant: Showtime Music Archive

Pg. 158-159 The Cash Cabin: Scott Petersen/Spdzine

Pg. 160 Johnny Cash: Showtime Music Archive/Colin Escott

Pg. 162-163 Johnny Cash: Showtime Music Archive/Colin Escott

Pg. 164-165 Johnny Cash: Showtime Music Archive/Colin Escott Johnny Cash/Sun Record: Sun Entertainment , Inc.

Pg. 166 Johnny Cash Record: Showtime Music Archive

Pg. 168-169 Johnny Cash Albums: Showtime Music Archive

Pg. 170-171 Johnny Cash Performing: Showtime Music Archive/Colin Escott

Pg. 173 Johnny Cash: Showtime Music Archive/Colin Escott

Pg. 174 Johnny Cash: Performing: Showtime Music Archive

Pg. 176 Johnny Cash: Showtime Music Archive

Pg. 178 Jerry Lee Lewis: Showtime Music Archive/Bill Millar/Colin Escott

Pg. 180 Jerry Lee Lewis: Showtime Music Archive

Pg. 182 Jerry Lee Lewis: Showtime Music Archive

Pg. 184-185 Jerry Lee Lewis and Linda Gail Lewis: Showtime Music Archive/Colin Escott

Pg. 186 Jerry Lee Lewis: Showtime Music Archive

Pg. 188 Jerry Lee Lewis: Showtime Music Archive

Billboard Ad: Showtime Music Archive

Pg. 190-191 Jerry Lee Lewis: Showtime Music Archive

Pg. 193 Jerry Lee Lewis: Showtime Music Archive

Pg. 194 Jerry Lee Lewis Album: Showtime Music Archive

Pg. 194-195 Jerry Lee Lewis Records: Sun Entertainment , Inc.

Pg. 196 Jerry Lee Lewis and Myra Gale Brown: Showtime Music Archive/Colin Escott

Pg. 197 Jerry Lee Lewis and Myra Gale Brown: Showtime Music Archive/Colin Escott

Pg. 199 Jerry Lee Lewis and Band: Jerry Lee Lewis and Myra Gale Brown: Showtime Music Archive/Colin Escott/Roland Janes

Pg. 200 Jerry Lee Lewis: Showtime Music Archive/Colin Escott

CHAPTER 5

Pg. 204 Tillman Franks and Johnny Horton: Showtime Music Archive/Colin Escott

Johnny Horton Abbot Flyer: Showtime Music Archive/Colin Escott

Pg. 206 Johnny Horton and Elvis: Showtime Music Archive/Colin Escott

Johnny Horton: Showtime Music Archive

Johnny Horton and Johnny Cash: Showtime Music Archive/Colin Escott

Pg. 207 Johnny Horton Performing: Showtime Music Archive/Colin Escott

Pg. 208 Johnny Horton: Showtime Music Archive

Pg. 211 Johnny Cash and Johnny Horton: Showtime Music Archive/Colin Escott

Pg. 213 Johnny Horton: Showtime Music Archive/Colin Escott

Pg. 214-215 Gene Vincent performing: Red Robinson Mangement

Pg. 217 Gene Vincent: Showtime Music Archive

Pg. 218 Gene Vincent and the Blue Caps: Showtime Music Archive

Pg. 220 Gene Vincent Smoking: Showtime Music Archive

Gene Vincent Performing: Showtime Music Archive

Pg. 221 Gene Vincent and the Blue Caps: Showtime Music Archive

Pg. 223 Gene Vincent: Showtime Music Archive

Pg. 224 Buddy Knox: Buddy Wayne Knox Estate

Pg. 226 Buddy Knox and Band: Buddy Wayne Knox Estate

Pg. 229 Buddy Knox: Buddy Wayne Knox Estate

Pg. 230 Buddy Knox: Buddy Wayne Knox Estate

Pg. 232 Buddy Knox: Showtime Music Archive

Pg. 234-235 Buddy Knox and Pontiac: Buddy Wayne Knox Estate

Pg. 237 Buddy Knox Promo: Showtime Music Archive

Pg. 239 Buddy Knox: Showtime Music Archive

Pg. 240 Bob Luman and the Shadows: Showtime Music Archive

Pg. 242 Elvis Presley: Showtime Music Archive

Pg. 243 Bob Luman on stage: Joseph Kent Jr./Louisianna Hayride Inc

EPILOGUE

Pg. 244 Bob Luman: Showtime Music Archive

Pg. 246 Bob Luman on stage: Joseph Kent Jr./Louisianna Hayride Inc

Bob Luman and Red Robinson: Red Robinson Mangement

Pg. 247 Bob Luman: Showtime Music Archive

Pg. 249 Bob Luman: Showtime Music Archive

Pg. 250-251 Charlie Rich Piano: Showtime Music Archive/Colin Escott

Pg. 253 Charlie Rich Piano: Showtime Music Archive/Colin Escott

Pg. 254 Charlie Rich and family: Showtime Music Archive/Colin Escott

Pg. 256-257 Charlie Rich recording: Showtime Music Archive/Colin Escott

Pg. 259 Charlie Rich: Showtime Music Archive/Colin Escott

Pg. 260 Howlin' Wolf: Showtime Music Archive

Pg. 261 Johnny Burnett Singing: Showtime Music Archive

Burnett Trio: Showtime Music Archive/Colin Escott

Burnett Trio: Showtime Music Archive/Colin Escott

Pg. 262 Johnny Burnett: Showtime Music Archive/Colin Escott

Boxing Gloves: antiquemystique.com

Pg. 265 Johnny Burnett Small Stage: Showtime Music Archive/Colin Escott

Pg. 266 Dorsey Burnett: Showtime Music Archive

Pg. 267 Dorsey Burnett: Showtime Music Archive/Colin Escott

Pg. 270 Johnny Burnett: Showtime Music Archive/Colin Escott

Pg. 271 Dorsey Burnett: Showtime Music Archive

Pg. 272-273 Elvis Presley: Showtime Music Archive/Colin Escott

Pg. 274 Elvis Presley: Showtime Music Archive

Pg. 256 1958 Hayride Picture; Jerry Naylor Company LLC

Pg. 258-259 American Flag: turbophoto.com

Pg. 266-267 Jerry Naylor, Patrick McGuire and Stan Perkins: Jerry Naylor Company LLC; Jerry Naylor and Glen Campbell: Jerry Naylor Company LLC; Jerry Naylor and Kris Kristofferson: Scott Petersen

ALSO AVAILABLE

THE ROCKABILLY LEGENDS: A TRIBUTE TO MY FRIENDS

This two-hour-and-forty-five-minute feature documentary takes you on a unique journey from the roots of Rockabilly in the Depression-era cotton fields and rural churches of Arkansas, Tennessee, and Texas, into the juke joints, honky-tonks, and recording studios of the urban South, and finally onto the world's stage as it gives birth to rock and roll. Listen as you hear this compelling story from the lips of the pioneering Legends themselves—Elvis Presley, Carl Perkins, Johnny Cash, Roy Orbison, Jerry Lee Lewis, Buddy Holly, Buddy Knox, Gene Vincent, Johnny Horton, Bob Luman, Charlie Rich, The Johnny Burnette Trio, and more. The documentary features a cinematic treasury of vintage live performances by the Legends, classic photographs and never-before-broadcast interviews with them, as well as exclusive commentary from friends, family, musicians, and producers of the founding fathers of fifties rock and roll/Rockabilly. Immerse yourself in the story of the birth of a music revolution through The Rockabilly Legends.

The documentary is co-hosted by Jerry Naylor and award-winning radio and television host, Red Robinson, while the story is masterfully narrated by game show pioneer and television icon Wink Martindale.

THE 4-CD SOUNDTRACK SET

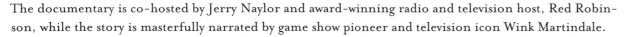

On these newly recorded documentary soundtrack masters, Jerry Naylor pays tribute to the Rockabilly Legends and the musical genres where Rockabilly had its roots—African-American spirituals and slave songs, delta blues, Southern gospel, bluegrass and hillbilly music. Recorded at Patrick McGuire Recording in Arlington, Texas, with an all-star band, each track reveals Rockabilly passion like never before.

For almost two years, Jerry Naylor and Carl Stanley Perkins, son of the iconic Carl Perkins, created, wrote, and recorded a passionate tribute to the godfather of Rockabilly. Stan's second-generation Rockabilly performance reveals the heavy influence of his father's unique vocal performance, with that Carl Perkins pushy rock-blues lead guitar style. The Perkins-Naylor duet vocals bring new, fresh excitement to the classic Carl Perkins songs. Featuring fifty-one extraordinary new masters of fifties rock.

TRIBUTE TO THE ROCKABILLY LEGENDS: VOLUMES 1–8

These compilation CDs are filled with one hundred and thirteen original master recordings of the best-known Rockabilly Legends's hits, each digitally refurbished and restored exclusively for this memorable collection. These songs sound as powerful and fresh as the day they were first recorded. Each of the eight compilation discs contains a rare bonus track carefully chosen for this Rockabilly Legends collection from live performances by The Everly Brothers, Bill Haley & The Comets, and Gene Vincent, as well as a colorful ten-page CD booklet.

TRIBUTE TO THE ROCKABILLY LEGENDS: LIVE ON THE LOUISIANA HAYRIDE

Contains unforgettable 1950s live performances by Elvis Presley, Johnny Cash, Johnny Horton, Bob Luman and Hank Williams, from the historic stage of the Louisiana Hayride. This amazing collection includes Elvis Presley's first performance on the Hayride in October 1954, as well as Hank Williams' final Hayride performance before his death.

TRIBUTE TO THE ROCKABILLY LEGENDS: RED ROBINSON CONVERSATIONS WITH THE LEGENDS

Legendary DJ Red Robinson—inductee to the Rock and Roll Hall of Fame, Rockabilly Hall of Fame, British Columbia Entertainment Hall of Fame and Canadian Association of Broadcasters Hall of Fame—shares his no-holds-barred interviews with Johnny Cash, Elvis Presley, Carl Perkins, Roy Orbison, Jerry Lee Lewis, and Charlie Rich.

ACKNOWLEDGMENTS

Thanks to:

- Wink and Sandy Martindale for introducing me to John Cerullo and Hal Leonard Publishing.

- Tommy Overstreet for faithfully managing the multi-layered details of this creative effort.

- Jason Ritchie and Tom Bert for sharing this Tribute to the Rockabilly Legends dream with us as co-executive producers of the project.

- A very special thank you to Scott Petersen and Jonah Nolde who ingeniously created all of the artistic graphic design and classic photographic imagery which is sure to make our Rockabilly story a collectable.

Finally, a special thank you to John Cerullo and his dedicated staff at Hal Leonard Trade Books, Amadeus Press, and Limelight Editions. I'm grateful for your support and your belief in our story and in this project.

CUSTOM DOCUMENTARY DVD

This exclusive documentary, custom-made to accompany the book *The Rockabilly Legends: They Called It Rockabilly Long Before They Called It Rock and Roll*, instantly takes you back to the rollicking era that witnessed the birth of fifties rock and roll. Kris Kristofferson welcomes you to join him in reliving that magical time when innovators with names like Presley, Cash, Holly, and Orbison lit up the entertainment world with their new brand of raw, infectious music. This DVD features full-length vintage performances from Elvis Presley, Carl Perkins, Johnny Cash, Jerry Lee Lewis, and Buddy Holly, not seen in the original three-hour feature documentary on which this version is based. It also includes a special appearance from Johnny Cash's son, John Carter Cash. You'll be delighted to hear the Rockabilly Legends, in their own words, tell the fascinating story of how their immortal music came to be. Just like the book, this custom DVD is destined to become a collector's dream.